TOZER SPEAKS TO STUDENTS

TOZER

SPEAKS *to*

STUDENTS

CHAPEL MESSAGES
PREACHED AT
WHEATON COLLEGE

Edited with an Introduction by
LYLE W. DORSETT

CAMP HILL, PENNSYLVANIA

Christian Publications, Inc.
3825 Hartzdale Drive, Camp Hill, PA 17011
www.cpi-horizon.com

Faithful, biblical publishing since 1883

ISBN: 0-87509-747-2
© 1998 by Christian Publications
All rights reserved
Printed in the United States of America

98 99 00 01 02   5 4 3 2 1

Cover photo courtesy of
Messiah College, Grantham, PA

CONTENTS

INTRODUCTION

As a historian I am always digging through library archives, searching for documents in out-of-the-way places and tracking down people who might remember the times, events and people I intend to write about. Recently my attention has been focused on A.W. Tozer. Except for C.S. Lewis and perhaps Oswald Chambers, it is difficult to find a twentieth-century Protestant author who has a wider audience than Tozer. Best known for such classics as *The Knowledge of the Holy* and *The Pursuit of God*, Tozer wrote numerous books during his lifetime. Since his death in 1963, many of his sermons, as well as editorials he wrote for *The Alliance Weekly* (now *Alliance Life*), have been dusted off, transcribed and published in book form. Indeed, a century after his birth—he was born in 1897—over forty titles bearing Tozer's name are in print. These works are widely circulated, frequently quoted from pulpits and platforms and often used to illustrate points made by countless writers of books, articles and missionary letters.

If it is rather common knowledge that A.W. Tozer wrote well and his books continue to find a wide readership, it is less well known that he had a particularly profound impact on college students. Like D.L. Moody, who ministered in the late nineteenth century, Tozer had a keen sense of his calling to encourage and equip young people to glorify God and fulfill the Great Commission.

The impetus for this concern can be traced to his own pilgrimage. Tozer heard a call to ministry while a teenager. Converted at age seventeen, this farm lad who had been educated in a country schoolhouse immediately embarked upon a rigorous program of Bible study and devotional reading. Along the path to full-time pastoral ministry, a few people encouraged young Tozer, pointed him to good books and taught him to seek an intensely deep and personal relationship with the Lord Jesus Christ.

The efforts of these saints were well directed. Tozer took his first church—a small Christian and Missionary Alliance church—in West Virginia when he was barely old enough to vote. A decade and three pastorates later, Tozer arrived to fill the pulpit of Chicago's South Side Alliance Church.

It was there, beginning in 1928, that this young minister without the benefit of extensive formal schooling began to go out of his way to encourage young people called to career ministry. From the late 1920s until he moved to Toronto in 1959, Tozer targeted students at Moody Bible Institute (MBI). He frequently spoke at MBI, and his church was always open to students from the institute. Over the years a steady stream of young people made their way to Tozer's Alliance church—a place where they were welcomed, inspired and taught biblical truth by a man whose preaching set them ablaze.

By the 1940s A.W. Tozer had become close friends with Dr. V. Raymond Edman, a dedicated Alliance man with a Ph.D. in history. Edman fully embraced the Alliance pillars of Jesus Christ as Savior, Sanctifier, Healer and Coming King. Paying more than lip service to these truths, this college professor, who served as President of Wheaton College from 1941 through 1964, stood committed to the deeper life. He had personally experienced a transformational work of grace after his conversion. He also knew from church history and personal experience that the Spirit of Jesus Christ wants to work and flow through men and women in profound, God-glorifying ways that are seldom realized by committed Christians.

Tozer and Edman became close friends. Among the consequences of this relationship were regular invitations to Dr. Tozer to interact with Wheaton College students, particularly as a chapel speaker. A year seldom passed during the post-World War II years without Tozer speaking at Wheaton College's Pierce Chapel.

There is no way to measure Tozer's influence on college students, but it must have been enormous. Several sources I have uncovered reveal that next to Dr. Edman, the most popular speaker at Wheaton College during the 1940s and 1950s was Tozer. "We loved to hear him preach," one former student recalled. "He enthralled us," said another, "because he spoke with a different voice."

Tozer seemed like a breath of fresh air to these young people for several reasons. First, he avoided the stained-glass voice. He loathed pompous-sounding God-talk, and he absolutely refused to use hackneyed fundamentalist and evangelical jargon. Second, Tozer loved words. He was a splendid communicator, and he excelled at presenting biblical truth in clear ways replete with vivid illustrations.

Tozer also intrigued his college audiences because of his transparency. He admitted his shortcomings and he preached on what he personally had experienced from biblical truth and his intimate relationship with Christ. These discerning students knew the difference between men who could exegete Scripture and those whose hearts had been truly changed by the Bible.

Another reason why Tozer's words flowed with ease through Wheaton chapel audiences can be attributed to his lack of a traditional theological education. To be sure, an ignorant speaker is apt to offend or bore a congregation of college women and men. But Tozer's mind was neither empty nor undisciplined. Although he preached without the benefit of Bible school, college or seminary training, his head was full of years of self-directed education. The man who only had about eleven years of formal schooling steeped himself in history, theology, poetry and philosophy. He drank deeply from the rich nectar of the early church fathers and his knowledge of deeper-life writers, whose works spanned centuries of church history, would have impressed the finest historians of ancient and medieval church history.

Tozer introduced college people to writers they had never read. He likewise shared stories with them of mystical experiences—stories that stirred young people's hearts. In brief, when Tozer set foot on the Wheaton College campus, student expectations ran high. People expected to be intellectually stimulated and spiritually inspired and they were not disappointed.

A.W. Tozer had properly diagnosed the condition of the Church in post-war America. People cried out for spiritual food, but they were not being fed. Heads were full of doctrine and biblical truth, but hearts were cold and spirits were comatose. "We need a revival of personal heart religion," he cried. The president of Wheaton College agreed, and so did the students.

Of course there were critics. One faculty member at Wheaton College confronted Tozer after a chapel with no intentions of complimenting the preacher. He said: "Tozer, you're a bit of a mystic, aren't you?" Tozer's reply delighted students: "Of course I'm a mystic. How else can you have a personal relationship with Jesus Christ today?"

In many ways Tozer's messages are just as timely now as they were a generation ago. In the following pages, eleven of A.W. Tozer's messages to Wheaton College students are published for the first time since he preached them in the early 1950s. The first sermon was delivered in chapel in February, 1952. The next nine messages comprise a week of evangelistic services given during autumn 1952. The concluding sermon was presented at Pierce Chapel on March 4, 1954.

Upon discovering these sermons, I was convinced that Brother Tozer had spoken words that are as appropriate for college students today as they were a half century ago. If he could speak to university men and women today, I think he would want to convey the same timeless truths. It is my prayer that he will speak to you with the same life-changing power that he spoke to his generation.

Lyle W. Dorsett
Wheaton College
Wheaton, Illinois
July 1998

CHAPTER

1

Spiritual Power

"Ye shall receive power . . ." (Acts 1:8). Those four words are the promise our Lord Jesus Christ gave to His waiting disciples. The word "power" in our English language may mean a number of things; particularly, it may mean one of two: *authority to do* or *ability to do*. When our Lord used the word "power," He meant "Ye shall receive ability to do." So what our Lord actually promised to His disciples was a spiritual potency enabling them to do *something*—He did not say what. "Ye shall receive ability to do"—the sentence dangles; we have to piece it out by the rest of the Scriptures and by the rest of the truth our Lord taught us.

This spiritual potency, this supernatural visitation which He said was to come upon them, was to be an invasion from beyond them. It was to come into their personalities from outside, from somewhere beyond and above, from a realm in which they had not previously lived and with which they had not been previously experientially acquainted. Here is the great gulf that separates Christianity from every quasi-religion.

We have, God knows, a world of them: Bahaism, New Thought, Unity, yoga, various forms of applied psychology, auto-suggestion and all the rest. And they all say the same thing and attempt the same thing: to wake up something, to tap the hidden powers inside of us. In their books they popularize their doctrines by such silly phrases as "wake the sleeping giant within you" and "tune in to your hidden potentials." Since nobody knows what any of those things mean, they buy their books, of course, and join their religions.

They tell us also to "learn to think creatively." All you have to do these days in order to make a lot of money is to write a book on any of these topics: "How to Quiet Your Mind," "How to Wake Your Solar Plexus" or "How to Arouse the Giant That Lies Dormant within You."

All these concepts are based upon the assumption that man is all right to start with—he's simply asleep; he needs to be awakened. Somewhere there is a terrific reservoir of moral power; if he can only get that awake somehow, if he can tune into it, if he can plug into his potentialities, he will be a wonderful fellow.

I do not say that these things do not help some. I suppose a poor little henpecked man on his way home from work does need a bit of a jacking up like that. For a man who has been pushed around all day and is on his way home to get pushed around some more, anything that will make that man feel he is somebody—I suppose it does him some human good.

But that is the great gulf that separates true biblical Christianity from any other teaching in the wide world. Christianity says, "Ye shall receive power," that is, moral ability to do. There is a potency to enter your nature from another world, a moral and spiritual force which is to come to you through faith. And it is to enable you to be not what the books say you should be, but what God says you should be, and to enable you to be what you want to be.

This invasion of our weakness from without is the beating heart of the moral side of Christianity. And that is the reason that all forms of ethical Christianity are inadequate. There are really many forms of ethical Christianity, humanism being one of them; they all assume, I repeat, the same thing. The assumption is that we are all right if we only think so.

A man came to this country years ago, and he got a lot of publicity and many followers by having a little sort of a homemade rosary. This little string with knots on it was all you had to have, and you woke in the morning and said five or ten times, "Every day in every way I am getting better and better."

Christianity knows nothing about this at all. We go beyond that; we go deeper than that. Jesus says, "Ye shall receive power"—a potent force from another world, invading your life by your consent, getting to the roots of your life and transforming you into His likeness. That is the teaching of our Lord Jesus Christ.

What is this power? "Ye shall receive power, after that the Holy Ghost is come upon you. . . ." This is the power of the Holy Spirit. This is not like the occult. I wish I could make all of God's children understand that there is nothing weird or uncanny about the Holy Spirit, nothing strange, nothing abnormal, nothing that sends shivers up your spine or makes you feel you've seen a ghost; nothing of that eeriness about the Holy Spirit. The Holy Spirit is the Spirit of Jesus; the Holy Spirit is exactly like Jesus, for what Jesus was, He was by the power of the Spirit, so that when we have the Holy Spirit, we have Jesus Christ.

I might say, claiming no theological or meta-physical accuracy, that the Holy Ghost is deity in solution. All that God the Father is, and all that God the Son is, the Holy Ghost is; He is nothing more and nothing less. So that when Jesus said, "Ye shall receive power," He simply meant that "All that my Father is and all that I am, by spiri-tual potency, is to be made available to you in the person of the Holy Ghost."

The Spirit of God is greatly neglected in our times; He's crowded into a paragraph in the books on sys-tematic theology, or He is carefully apologized for by people who are afraid of fanaticism. That is a trick of the devil to frighten people away from this potency which is the essence of Christianity.

How does this power operate? I do not know that I can tell you, but I might help you understand by say-ing that the power of the Holy Spirit operating in the human heart is an unmediating force applied directly to the spirit of the individual—the human spirit.

You and I are spirits. We are spirits that have bodies. We are different from the beasts in that they just have bodies. We are different from angels in that they are spirits without bodies (I presume they are; I know little about them, but I have guessed that much). But you and I are spirits to whom God has given a body.

William Jennings Bryan,[1] in his great oration on the Prince of Peace, referred to the fact that our souls are simply "guest royal come from afar to inhabit a little while" what he called this "tenement of clay." And thus, we are spirits. Beyond your mentality, beyond your soul where aesthetic beauty such as Bach and Beethoven are felt and appreciated, beyond all this and even deeper is where the Spirit of God wants to go.

It is my conviction that we are overdue for a revival of inwardness—not a revival of sitting around looking at our thumbs or sitting like a statue of Buddha, but a revival of appreciation of the inwardness of true spiritual Christianity. The Spirit of power that comes from God to redeemed men's hearts is a power that operates directly and unmediated upon us from Spirit to spirit.

A wrestler achieves his success by pressure of body upon body, and a teacher achieves his success by the pressure of ideas on the mind. The moralist achieves his success by the pressure of obligation upon conscience, but the Spirit of God achieves His end by the pressure of Himself deep within the spirit of man.

There is an old word used by some of the writers of medieval times—you do not hear it anymore, although it is still found in the dictionary—it is the word *penetralia*. They talked about God in the *penetralia*. I do not know all the word means, but I would assume it would mean that place which you must *penetrate* to—that deep place within you, deeper even than the mind can go. And it is there that the Spirit of God works. He works in the *penetralia*, in the sanctum deep within, that which is merely of our bodies or souls or minds.

I do not say that the Holy Ghost does not make use of other means because, after all, we are physical. I do not say that He does not make use of our minds, because He most certainly does. God has equipped us with minds, and I for one belong to that company of fundamentalists who are not adverse to thinking. I do not believe that there is any basic incompatibility between a good mind and a good heart. I do not believe that we must be dumb to be happy. I do not mean, necessarily, that intellectuality makes you good, but it does not hurt you any if you know what to do with it. But I do say that the Spirit of God does use the human mind. I believe that one of the most beautiful things in the world is a sanctified mentality, a good, sharp mind, broad and high and noble and lofty and yet keen as a razor, that is anointed with the Spirit of God to give it tenderness, love, purity and fineness.

Someone said the other day in one of our newspapers, "Why is it that Alexander Pope is unquestionably one of the most skillful of all the English poets, yet is one of the least loved of all the English poets?" Then he answered his own question; he said it is because he lacked that one essential element—love. He had a tremendous intellect, but nobody liked the man somehow. You read and quote what he has to say, sort of at arm's length; there are never any pulsations there, never any warm attraction because the man lacked love.

An intellect without this inward potency to lay hold of it may be a very destructive thing and something that we do not take much pleasure in. The company of a fine mind may be a very embarrassing matter unless that mind has been anointed with the soft, sweet oil of the Holy Ghost so there is love and charity and understanding. So I do not say that the Spirit of God never makes use of these means. I most assuredly say that He does, but the deep inner sanctuary is beyond all means.

When Jesus said, "Ye shall receive power," He meant you shall receive the pressure of the Spirit of God upon the heart, upon the spirit. How the Spirit works, again I say I do not know, I cannot tell you. I can only describe an experience, but I can never explain it.

There are those who shy away from Christianity because of what they call its mystic element; they say it cannot be explained. My stock answer to all such objectors is that all of us live habitually all the time. All of us—from the horse meat manufacturers on up to the saints—we live by things that we do not understand. Up and down the scale—every gangster, every mother, every simple person in the woods of Kentucky—everybody lives by things we cannot understand. We cannot understand life; we cannot understand love; we cannot understand light. We just take it all for granted and live by it.

So when they tell me, "Aw, get away with it; I do not believe in any mystic element in Christianity, any of that mysterious power you are talking about because I cannot understand it," I reply, "I cannot understand life, but I am alive. I cannot understand love, but I love a lot of people. I cannot understand all this, but I can only know how it works and I can experience it."

This power that comes to the human breast by faith does not create objects. That is where imagination and all sorts of weird, occult religions come in. They create things that do not exist, but the Holy Spirit never creates anything that does not exist. He simply lifts the fog off it and shows it to us. He does not create the mountain; He takes away the shroud from the mountain so that it stands clear and bright in the sunshine. The Holy Spirit comes giving us inward understanding so that in one sense, "Ye need not that any man teach you: but as the same anointing teacheth you of all things . . ." (1 John 2:27).

By that He does not exclude teachers; that same Holy Ghost creates teachers, makes them and sets them in the Church. But He did say that He was going to teach us at a deeper level than our human intellect; He is going to inform us farther in than we can be informed by the words of a man or by a book; He's going into the *penetralia*. "Ye shall receive power," and that is ability to do and power to perform.

Therein lies the throbbing powerhouse of Christianity. It is the invasion; it is the Person that has come in from beyond us, lost as we were in sin, and has brought that potency, that ability to achieve moral ends, inside of us. After that, Christianity ceases to be an ethical thing at all and it becomes a spiritual reality. Then it lays hold of ethics; it lays hold of these external things, transforms them and glorifies them.

The Holy Ghost reveals objects present, things unknown and unseen. Above all things the business of the Spirit of God in its fullest effectiveness is to remove the veil from the soul and show us Jesus Christ. "He shall take of mine, and shall show it unto you" (John 16:15). Jesus Christ may simply be a historical Jesus, a theological Jesus or a philosophical Jesus until the Holy Spirit, that potency that enables within, reveals Him for what He is. Then we throw up our hands and cry, "My Lord and my God!"

He is the Jesus of history, most surely He is, but He is more than the Jesus of history. He is the Jesus of my heart; He is the present Christ. But He will never be known as that until it is by the power of the Spirit, for Paul says that no man can even call Jesus Lord except by the power of the Holy Ghost (1 Corinthians 12:3).

I would suppose Paul means to call Jesus Lord so as to be acceptable before God. Anybody can call Jesus "Lord" and not be saved—He said so Himself. But the power to know Jesus Christ Himself, the second Person of the Trinity, the divine Christ, depends upon the enabling of the Spirit of God within us.

It is my belief that the forgotten, or at least neglected, doctrine of our day, the most important one of them all after atonement itself, is that we, as God s redeemed people, have a right to expect and receive from Him by faith a power that will do in us what all the poor religions of the world can never do. This power will bring to us the shining face of Jesus and make Him real within us, so that not only the moral, theological and ethical qualities are present, but also the *mystical* quality—the sight of the face of Jesus Christ within the human breast.

There is not a lovelier sight. May God grant that we may understand this, believe it and enter into it.

[This message was delivered at a Wheaton College chapel service on February 28, 1952.]

CHAPTER

2

Preparing the Way
for the Lord

Now in the fifteenth year of the reign of Tiberius Caesar, Pontius Pilate, being governor of Judea, and Herod being tetrarch of Galilee, and his brother Philip tetrarch of Iturea and of the region of Trachonitis, and Lysanias the tetrarch of Abilene, Annas and Caiaphas being the high priests, the word of God came unto John the son of Zacharias in the wilderness. And he came into all the country about Jordan, preaching the baptism of repentance for the remission of sins; As it is written in the book of the words of Esaias the prophet, saying, The voice of one crying out in the wilderness, Prepare ye the way of Lord, make His paths straight. Every valley shall be filled, and every mountain and hill shall be brought low; and the crooked places shall be made straight, and the rough ways shall be made smooth; And all flesh shall see the salvation of God. (Luke 3:1-6)

Prepare ye the way of the Lord. These words were spoken by a man of God in a particular time; it has a particular and specific historic setting, and it can be understood that way.

God was preparing a people for the greatest event that ever took place in this world—the manifestation of the Messiah. In order to do that He had to prepare the people morally to understand Him and to receive Him.

That is the historic setting, but remember these words also have application for today because they constitute a spiritual principle which God has laid down and from which He has never varied during the centuries. It is always that way. If God is preparing to bless a man, that man has to get ready.

I know that will shock some people because there is a badly conceived theory abroad that God does it all; all you and I have to do is be born. After that God just picks us up on eagle wings and sweeps us irresistibly through to the crown at last. I cannot imagine how such a notion could ever have lodged itself in heads as small as ours are, but it is there. Consequently, it is necessary to point out that this is an error and that the principle of God's operation is that when He is about to do something unusual for a nation, a church, an individual, He gets that individual or nation or church morally ready. John was sent to do that very thing.

God wills certain things for people—spiritual prosperity, I might call it. Let me say that it consists of about two things: first, clear forgiveness of sin and washing from the same. God's will for everyone who hears the gospel is that we should be forgiven and thoroughly cleansed from sin. Second, we should be filled and walk in the fullness of the Holy Ghost all the days of our life. That will eventuate immediately, of course, fruitfulness, peace of heart, purity of life and general usefulness to our generation before we go hence to be no more.

This is not talk about a deluxe edition of a Christian. When I talk like this people often say: "Well, that is simply your extreme view of it. That is a deluxe, leather-bound edition, but do you not know that God has His paperbound editions too? The simple twenty-five-cent editions make up the great mass of Christians. They will get in; they are all right too. It is all right for mystics, hermits and certain ones such as Dr. A.B. Simpson,[1] Charles Wesley[2] or some other saint to rise to spiritual heights, but for us that is all out. We are too busy; we have too much to do and besides, we are living in a different generation."

If you feel that way about it there is not much that I can say that will help you. I hope you know better than that, because a Spirit-filled Christian is not a deluxe edition; he is a normal Christian. If he is anything less he is sick. A normal Christian is a person whose sins have been forgiven, who has not only a theological knowledge that his sins have been forgiven, but has also a deep consciousness of it. This is not an unusual Christian, or he ought not to be.

The old writers used to talk about "restored moral innocence." They said there are two ways to be innocent: one is never to have done it; the second is, having done it, to be so forgiven of God that you have no sense of ever having done it to the extent that you have restored moral innocence given to you by God. I believe this.

There are many of us that have gotten converted the hard way. We got picked out of the shell and our belief in our having salvation rests upon a conclusion drawn from a text. We have been made to believe that that is faith. I read a certain text and I draw a certain conclusion from it. I say, "Well, that is it. Now, let us go have a soda." That is about as deep as many of us go.

The forgiveness in the blood of Jesus Christ is a profounder thing than that! It is profounder than a conclusion drawn from biblical promises. It goes in to the depths of the spirit, it restores a sense of everlasting well-being, and it gives to the heart restored moral innocence. God means it to be for every one of us so that we can say,

> My God has reconciled,
> His pardoning voice I hear;
> He owns me for His child,
> I need no longer fear.[3]

My spirit answers and tells me I am born of God. God wills this condition for every one of His children. But do you know there is a difference between one who is forgiven theologically and one who is forgiven actually? There is a difference in the whole lift of his spirit, his countenance, the quality and tone of his testimony, his approach to life, others and God, and a difference in his prayer life.

God wills that we should be Spirit-filled Christians, walking in the fullness of His Spirit. You do not have to coax God into a good humor; we do not have to pray all night to get God coaxed up to do it for us. This is what the old camp-meeting brethren called "the purchase of the blood." All this is ours by blood right! He died and rose again the third day and ascended to God the Father Almighty. It was all done. We can add nothing to it. Utter spiritual prosperity, the tree in full bloom, the field in full grain—this is the will of God for His people.

When we say we are going to have a revival, what do we mean? We inadvertently admit that we are spiritually below par. We unintentionally admit that we are badly in need of having brought to us these things which are all ours by the grace of God which is in Christ Jesus. Let us remember that when God prepares to bless a community, a church people or a group, first He has to get us ready.

How can we get ready? There is a great fallacy abroad that a lot of talk will do it. I have never believed much in talk, though I have talked now for thirty-five years. Talk is all right if you mean to walk along with your talk, but I suppose that there is no organization in the world that has quite as much talk associated with it as religion. Politics comes second. And very often there is not much more reality in our religious talk than there is in political talk.

I trust God that it is not true that a word once spoken never is recalled. I trust God that somewhere out in the waves of space all the words spoken in all the churches of the world since the crucifixion are not being recorded. Would it not be an unattractive universe to roam around in and be bumped into from all sides by endless barrages of religious words? And we have spoken so many words because we have done so few deeds. Great deeds require few words, and few deeds require a great many words. So when we want to get ready we begin to talk. It is part and parcel of our way of doing, I suppose, because we continue to do it.

There is also a notion that if we get very busy we will get blessed. I suppose American people are the busiest people in the world. Someone from the Orient once asked what American people do with the time they save. That question has never been answered. We screech to a stop from forty-seven plus miles an hour at a stale yellow light to go nowhere at all! We American people think we are highly cultured and educated. Actually, we are often like a big bunch of fools, for we do things that the Chinese would never do; we do things that the ancients would have smiled at.

Great people have always thought before they acted. American people seldom think; we have our thinking done for us and put in digest magazines so that we do not have to think. We have our religion dished out for us in fiction form so we never have to grasp an abstract idea. Abstractions are absolutely indispensable to any grasp of spiritual things, and yet we have it all done for us. The writers and printing presses are busy printing things for us "saintlets" who haven't mentality enough or character enough to really believe and meditate and contemplate and dream over high things until they get ahold of us.

These religious fiction writers always pick Shirley for the name of the girl in the story. I have often wondered about Shirley—how did she get so popular? And her boyfriend is always named Ned. I have seen so many of these books of fiction—Ned and Shirley. They go to a ballgame and hold their Testaments over their heads and say, "Praise the Lord! Hit a home run, Charles!" It is always so neat, and so Victorian and so completely unreal. But it takes our minds off God, heaven and hell, reality and death, the Holy Ghost, moral things and lost men. And that is the curse in the world and in the church.

We cannot talk our way out of this jam; we cannot talk our way into preparedness for the mighty inmoving of God upon us, and we cannot work our way into it either. We can run around the neighborhood giving out tracts, and that is a fine thing to do. I have done it and hope I never get too old to do it, but that will not help us either when it comes to this thing God wants to do for us.

This sudden restoration of moral innocence that gives the heart a sense of forgiveness and cleansing, this fullness of the Spirit that walks in the Holy Ghost and bears fruit unto righteousness—that is divine. Never by external activities and talk will it ever come. And the reason it has not come sooner is that there are certain moral blocks that prevent God from moving in. He wants to come, He wills to come in, but there are certain moral blocks that prevent the blessing—moral blocks in our hearts and in our conduct.

These blocks must be removed. Just as a blood clot gets into the heart and causes coronary thrombosis by preventing the full flow of blood, so there gets into the veins and arteries of Christians certain blocks.

The Lord says, "You know better than this. You have read your Bible, and you have it before you." Indeed, the glory of the Lord wants to break in upon you and show you what is wrong with you. But we are prone to hunt somebody up and take up some of their time to have them tell us that we are all right. We are always ready to overlook what we very obviously know is wrong with us. This is a moral block—something that is blocking out the incoming of God.

I believe that the Holy Ghost comes into a person's life, as Dr. A.B. Simpson said, like breathing in, without any effort on our part. If you were to break a light bulb, there would be a pop; it is a vacuum, and the atmosphere wants to rush in there. It cannot get in past the glass, but as soon as you break it, the air rushes in. You do not have to get on your knees and cry, "Oh atmosphere, please rush into this bulb!" Break it, and it will rush in. That is all you have to do. You do not have to wait around and talk and talk and talk.

I believe that God wants to move in that very same way. He wants to move in an unusual way—not unusual because it is strange, but unusual only because so few of us are blessed in this way.

The human heart is very deceitful and desperately wicked apart from the good grace of God, and we can cheat ourselves, living half a lifetime, growing old and gray and cheating our own hearts unless we become suddenly very, very honest. I pray that we might not try to play tricks on our own hearts. We know what is bothering us.

"Prepare *YE* the way of the Lord." Why is it that you cannot control your temper? Why is it? No, it was not your Irish mother. It was your devilish ancient ancestor who had that virus injected into his veins and so we all have it. I had an English father and a German mother, and I had a temper like blue lightning. I had to do something about that temper or it most certainly would have done something about me.

Why can you not get victory over it? Why must it always upset you and make a fool of you in company? And why must it spoil your testimony before your friends? These blocks are in our hearts. They are what we call dispositional sins, but they may also be in our conduct in external things. We have got to get rid of them.

I hope you do not want anybody to baby you and say, "All right now, let us not take this too seriously; all is well." Let us not think of it like that. If all were well, you would not be half dead and you would not need the revival for which you have been praying. The fact is, all is *not* well, and we must have help here. We must have a visitation of God to individual hearts.

I do not know that I can tell you too much about mass revivals. When I was a very young man I used to preach a great deal on mass revivals. I had read Finney and was quite an expert on the subject of mass revivals, but as I have gotten older I know less about it than I used to.

But I can tell you how an individual can get revived. I can tell you how an individual can have such a spiritual revival that it will mean a growth and a bursting out in spiritual life as wonderful as when Jesus healed the lame man (Matthew 9:2-8; Mark 2:3-12; Luke 5:17-26). You can come out of sickness into health, out of weakness into power, out of heavy conscience into a beautiful sense of forgiveness and innocence again.

You do not have to wait until so many sermons have been preached before this happens; it can happen to you now. That I *do* know. I am not able to answer the question of whether there will be a great world revival before Jesus comes, but I say that you can have all that revival can bring within a matter of hours or less if you will "Prepare ye the way of the Lord."

Let us look at those things which may be keeping us from individual revival. Let us just cruelly break them down, and not spare the horses.

Personal Friendships

Let us look at personal friendships. Maybe the reason I cannot get victory over my flesh and the reason I am not able to live a fruitful and victorious life is because I habitually run around with the wrong people.

It is my opinion, after careful observation, that the greatest hindrance to the spiritual progress of young people is bad friendships. After many years in the ministry, I have observed it. Some bright-faced fellow who decides in a sudden impulse as he hears the Word of God, "This is for me! I want to follow Christ!

I want to accept Him and believe Him!" You show him the way, and it looks all right. You think, "Here is another disciple for the Savior."

But he goes back to the same crowd he has been with. Maybe he mumbles a testimony and tries to compromise it, but it is the same old crowd. It is not very long until he is all cooled off. Instead of walking with the Lord, he is not, or if he is, he is making very little spiritual progress.

Bad friendships, I say, are a reason for our slow-down in spiritual growth. Let us decide this. You say, "You would not have me turn my back on my best friend!" Well, I will not answer that, but I will quote somebody else. "If any man come to me, and is not willing to give up father, and mother and friends and houses and homes and his life also, he cannot be my disciple" (Luke 14:26, author's paraphrase). Any friendship that slows you down is a bad friendship, and you ought to give it up, whether it is by telephone, by mail or in person.

Personal Habits

Then, let us look at personal habits. Do my habits honor God? I must search my heart. "Search ye," says the Holy Ghost—in effect, "prepare ye" my personal habits. Do they honor God? Do they help me or do they hinder me? As I look myself over as we should, my common sense tells, "Now, wait a minute here. That habit you have just cannot help you in the king-dom of God." You can excuse it, say it doesn't occur in the Scriptures, challenge somebody to find the text, but in your heart you know that it hinders you. "Prepare ye the way of the Lord" by removing that hindrance. Take it out of your life, whatever it is.

Moral Habits

Then there are my moral habits. Here is a little rule to know whether they are all right or not. Would I dare have them publicly known? Am I habitually practicing anything that I would not have publicly known? There are lots of things we do not do in public; common decency tells us that there are certain things that are to be done in private, but could I have everybody know my moral habits—what I am doing and how I am living, without embarrassment?

If I cannot answer "yes"—joyfully—to that question, then I know what is wrong with me. I do not have to go ask somebody or write the question- and-answer department of some Christian periodical. I have an answer on that—I know already. If I will not admit it, I am simply being dishonest with my own heart. I have secret habits that will not bear the light of the gospel. "My pastor does not dare know about that! My teacher does not dare know about that! I would not want my friends to know." Well, I cannot do a thing about that from here, because the Lord did not say, "Tozer, prepare the way for these people." He said, "Prepare *ye*," individually, each of you, "the way of the Lord."

Past Life

I think about my past life. Are all my sins forgiven? Sins may be forgotten and not forgiven. Some people have long memories, maybe, when it come to remembering the wrongs of others, but when it comes to themselves they quickly forget, and it falls into the lint and dust of things forgotten. Because they have forgotten it, they think God has forgotten it.

But they fail to take into account that this is a moral universe run according to moral laws, and God is a holy, moral God. He cannot sustain His own character and maintain His own reputation among created beings, and let anything get by. If there is an unpardoned sin anywhere, that unpardoned sin still stands against the perpetrator. You want all the wrongs righted as far as possible.

You say, "There he goes now! I knew he was a legalist. He is preaching restitution." Yes, I am preaching restitution. You see, it is so reasonable. Suppose that while brother McAfee[4] slept over where he and I stay, I sneaked out of bed, and stole a $10 bill out of his wallet, and then said, "Forgive me, God, for stealing this $10 bill. I am sorry, and I take the blood for it, and I will never take another $10 bill." Then I go out and buy myself some things with his $10 bill.

I ask you, do you think it is reasonable that I can go about preaching, praying, looking pious, being happy in God and get my prayers answered without restoring that $10? Never! I have to take that back and say, "Ray, I am sorry, I yielded to temptation and stole $10 from you. Here is the $10." Then after that I can smile again, and preach again.

I used to steal when I was a boy. I never robbed banks, but I stole things. After I got converted I went around giving them all back. I suppose people thought I was plain crazy. I remember once I stole a ride on a railroad train in a boxcar. One day I was seeking God, and something said to me, "Now how about your riding around on the B & O Railroad without paying?"

"All right, all right, I've ridden on what they called the 'possum belly, on the old flat car," I said. "I suppose the only thing to do is write in."

That sounded silly, and it was, I suppose, but I sat down and wrote to the passenger traffic manager in Baltimore. I said,

Dear Sir,

Some years ago I rode one of your freight trains into Pittsburgh, Pennsylvania. I do not know how much I owe you, but I am a Christian now and want to get this off my conscience. I am writing to ask you how much I owe.

I got a letter back, but I am sure that the gentlemen dictated it with his tongue in his cheek. He said,

Dear Sir,

I am very happy to know that you have become a Christian, and I am in receipt of the letter that tells me that you have bummed around on my railroad without paying. I appreciate your honesty in telling me so, but my answer is that you probably did not get very good service, and we have no rates applying to boxcars. Therefore, you may consider yourself forgiven.

I suppose there was a "ho-ho" that went up from the office when that letter went into the basket, but when I opened that yellow envelope with B & O's signature upon the left corner and read that I was forgiven, I knew everything was all right.

You think that is carrying it too far? Maybe so, but in this day when folks do not carry things far enough, if I am going to be a fanatic I want to be a fanatic in the right direction. Do you not also? If I am going too far, I want to go too far toward heaven instead of toward hell.

I believe in restitution, and I believe that there are some things that need to be straightened out in our past lives. When a thing has been forgiven by the blood of Christ, there are not devils enough in all the lost creation to dig it up. But God is our Father and we are His children, and in His household He wants a fair, honest, clean people. Though that sin is now gone, there is a certain relationship between individuals that ought to be straightened out, and that is where restitution comes in. It is not to save us; it is to lift the weight off our hearts and get the right relationships established between man and man.

When a thing has once been forgiven, it is forgiven, and that is the end of that as far as God is concerned, but if you know that you can pay it back from man to man, do that. David said this strange thing: "My goodness extendeth not to thee, but to the saints that are in the earth" (Psalm 16:2-3). All this restitution of straightening out with my friends and living right with my fellowman—it does not endear me to God—"My goodness extendeth not to God, but to the saints that are on the earth." I have got to live right with people.

I do not believe in promiscuous confession. If it has been forgiven and I know that confessing it to the public will not do any good, then I believe it ought to be put where God put it, under the blood and left there, world without end. But if any good can be done, if I can straighten it out, if I can put that $10 back in that man's wallet, then I ought to do it. A full confession must be made to God where I cannot make it to man. There are many sins that I have committed that I cannot confess to people for various reasons. But God forgives it all, and wherever it is possible we ought to maintain the right relationship, and that is always possible between individuals.

Relationships with Others

If I have caused hard feelings anywhere, I ought to go get that straightened out. You know this is the day of the smart aleck, the quip-artist and cynical people. We have fed too long on *The New Yorker* and the radio commentators, and we have become hard. I believe God wants His people to be tender people, quick to forgive and ask forgiveness.

Many of us, I suppose, are not blessed because we owe an apology to somebody. We ought to go to somebody and say, "So-and-so, I am sorry. I have said awfully mean things about you, and I have not liked you at all."

God has sent me around to a few people like that, including a man bigger than I was. I was afraid of him, and I thought maybe if I told him how I felt about him he would bowl me over, but he did not. He grabbed my hand and said, "It is all right; I never had anything against you."

If I had carried that down in my heart all these years—it was thirty years ago—I would still have that down in me festering. But I got it straightened out. So my relationship to other people does matter.

Relationship to God

As well, my relationship to God certainly does matter. I wonder if God is pleased with my service for Him, pleased with my worship, pleased with my obedience and pleased with my love of the Scriptures. Is God pleased? You see, we live in a triangle, and we cannot get out of it. God and myself and others—that is the everlasting triangle in which all God's people live. I have to maintain those three relationships and keep them right. It is an easy thing to do if we will be obedient and trust in God. My relationship to God is primary; my relationship to people is secondary; my relationship to myself comes third.

In conclusion, when the blocks are removed, when I have taken them away, then, it says here in the grand, beautiful, poetic language of Isaiah, "The glory of the LORD shall be revealed" (40:5). And that is revival, when the glory of the Lord is revealed. God will not debate this with you and me. If you do not like what I am saying, I cannot help that. I hope you do, but if you do not I cannot help it. Everybody has a monitor in his breast if he's a Christian. The Holy Ghost dwells there and draws the sharp line between right and wrong. Every man or woman, if they listen to the Holy Ghost within them, will know whether they are right or not. Everybody knows in his own heart whether his relationship to God and his fellow man is right. Everyone can know whether his personal habits are hindering him, whether his secret habits are pure enough to be known to the world, whether his past life is forgiven, and whether he has straightened up, so far as it is possible, his relationships to his fellow men.

You cannot get God over on our side at all on that; we have to come over to God's side. There is no such thing as coming to God, the Eternal One, and making terms. God makes the terms and you accept them, that is all. God never changes. God is not reconciled; rather, God is propitiated and man is reconciled because the change is not in God, the change is in me. God always remains the same, like the sun that shines, asking no questions, shining His Holy Grace upon mankind.

If you pull down the blinds, the sun cannot get in, and these blinds have been pulled down long enough in our hearts. Why not now? Are you interested in this revival, or is it just another thing you attend because it is interesting? Are you concerned for your own soul? Do you want something new from God? Do you want to enter in from the twilight into the sunlight? Do you want to move from half-spirituality into the full-blazing light of God's love and be a spiritual man or woman? Then let us be very frank and bold and honest. Let us look into our own hearts and our own lives and our own conduct fairly with the light of God's Word. If you find there that there are hindrances and blocks, let us courageously remove them. And without any urging on God's part, God will move in on your life and transform it wondrously.

[This sermon was an evangelistic message delivered at Wheaton College, Pierce Chapel, September 29, 1952.]

CHAPTER

3

Grieve Not the Holy Spirit

And grieve not the Holy Spirit of God, whereby ye are sealed unto the day of redemption. (Ephesians 4:30)

T he Holy Spirit is a member of the Trinity, one of the blessed Three, but He is the forgotten member in the day in which we live. The Spirit of the Lord is present in the world. This is taught in the Bible. One of the old wisdom books of the Apocrypha says, "The Spirit of the Lord fills the world." Just as our souls permeate our bodies and just as the air fills all space around the earth, so the blessed Holy Spirit is here.

You are never sinning alone; you are never grieving alone; you are never alone, for the Spirit of the Lord is here. He is nearer to us than our bodies and our breath—and He is God. He is not as ether or gravitation or energy, but He is one of the holy Godhead three. It is so taught all through Scripture that the divine Being consists of Father, Son and Holy Spirit. The Holy Spirit comes last in our formula, but there is no last in the Godhead. The Athanasian Creed states,

> And in this Trinity there is none before or af-
> ter; none is greater or less than another; but
> the whole three Persons are co-eternal to-
> gether and co-equal, so that in all things, as
> is aforesaid, the Unity in Trinity and the
> Trinity in Unity is to be worshiped.

The creeds of the church have always taught that the Holy Ghost is God, including the Apostle's Creed. And if they did not, it is still all through the Bible. The point is, we are not dealing with one another primarily, but we are dealing with God's Holy Spirit on earth. The Holy Spirit is here and has always been here.

It is inconceivable that there is any place where He could not be, but when He came after fifty days (see Acts 2), He came in a sense that He had not been before, manifesting Himself in a way that He had not before and carrying a commission that He had not had before. He is concerned with people; the Holy Ghost is concerned with you. He is here earnestly, eagerly and intimately concerned, work-ing in, for, toward and among, and He is in har-mony with the Father and Son. "Such as the Father is," says the Athanasian Creed,

> Such is the Son and such is the Holy
> Ghost. The Father uncreated, the Son un-
> created and the Holy Ghost uncreated; the
> Father incomprehensible, the Son incompre-
> hensible and the Holy Ghost incomprehensi-
> ble; the Father eternal, the Son eternal and

the Holy Ghost eternal. And yet there are not three Eternals, but one Eternal, as also not three Uncreated nor three Incomprehensibles, but one Uncreated and one Incomprehensible. So, likewise, the Father is almighty, the Son almighty and the Holy Ghost almighty; and yet not three Almighties, but one Almighty.

So the Father is God, the Son is God and the Holy Ghost is God; and yet not three Gods, but one God. So likewise the Father is Lord, the Son Lord and the Holy Ghost Lord. And yet not three Lords, but one Lord. For like as we are compelled by Christian truth to acknowledge every Person by Himself to be God and Lord, so are we forbidden by the catholic religion to say, There be three Gods or three Lords.

So the Holy Spirit is here working in harmony with the Book. He might do things you have not yet discovered in the Bible, for He wrote the Book. It is His Book, and it is the Word of the Father. It is the Book in print which is the revealed will of God, not on every subject, but on that pertaining to our salvation. There is much to learn that is not in the Bible, but there is nothing to learn pertaining to my everlasting welfare that is not in the Bible. The Holy Ghost will always teach according to the Book in harmony with the Father and the Son and in pursuance of the eternal purpose of God.

The Holy Ghost has sovereign right over us. I believe in the sovereignty of God. My definition of the sovereignty of God is simply God Almighty's freedom to do always all that He wills to do. This is the Holy Ghost—He's sovereign. He has the freedom and right to do all that He wills to do, and He will not be hindered. He is the creative power of our being and He holds our life in being by His presence. It says in Hebrews 1:3 that all things are held together by the Word of God, and the Holy Ghost, filling all space, is the adhesive element in the universe that holds it together. If God were to remove Himself from His creation, if that were possible, it would fall back into chaos and cease to be. The Holy Ghost is here and He has priority— remember that. The Holy Ghost has priority over your pastor, your church, your teachers—priority over every human thing. He is God, and being God, His voice has priority over all voices, His will over all wills and His instruction over all other instruction.

The Holy Spirit can be intimate and personal, and He insists upon being so. There is nothing that the Holy Spirit does not claim the right to examine and decide. The Holy Spirit is not interfering with my habits; He is doing His divine work when He deals with them. The Holy Ghost has the right to examine and decide my conduct, the flow of habits, whatever they are. When it becomes a chain of habits, it becomes conduct, so the Holy Spirit has the right to examine the flow and chain of habits that become conduct.

The Holy Ghost also has the perfect Sovereign right to decide on my friendships. Of all things that hinder Christian growth, I think bad friendships come close to the top. The Holy Ghost has a perfect right to decide my love life and to deal with marriage, ambitions, plans, possessions, destiny and all that I do. He claims and has the right to deal with, examine and decide whatever I do and what I am. That is the blessed Holy Spirit.

He is here, but He is the forgotten person of the Trinity. We deal with Him as politicians deal with Abraham Lincoln—we fall back on Him for a point or quote Him reverently, but we always think of Him as being somewhere else at some remote time. But neither "somewhere-elseness" nor "former-timeness" belongs to the Holy Ghost. The Holy Ghost is now and here.

The difference between unbelief and faith is the difference between there and here, between now and then. The unbeliever says, "I believe in God *there*." The believer says, "I believe in God *here*." The unbeliever says, "I believe in the Holy Ghost *then*." The believer says, "I believe in the Holy Ghost *now*." It is a difference between now and then, here and there.

Anybody can believe in the God of the day of Abraham. Anybody can believe in the Holy Ghost of the millennium. But believers believe in the Holy Ghost now. He is not just then, He is now; He is there, but He is also here. We are in His hands whether we like it or not—whatever our background or religious teaching might have been, whatever excesses might have been clustered around the teaching and practice of the Holy Ghost, we cannot escape the fact that we are in the hands of the Holy Spirit.

This is the dispensation of the Holy Spirit. You cannot know Jesus Christ except as the Holy Ghost reveals Him unto you. You, by your fall in Adam, were altogether blind. You can know about the history of Jesus, but you can never know Jesus except as the Holy Spirit makes Him real to you.

We cannot afford to ignore the Holy Ghost. We cannot afford to let Him continue to be the forgotten member of the Trinity. We must give Him the place our fathers gave Him, the place the Bible gives Him, the place that He holds by virtue of the fact that He is one with the Father and the Son, one in eternity, one in substance, one in glory and one in majesty.

How We Treat the Holy Spirit

How do we treat this Holy Spirit? We can blaspheme the Holy Spirit. This is extreme irreverence toward Him—scurrilous thoughts and scurrilous remarks and indignity offered to His Holy Person. As far as I know, there are only two passages in the Bible that tell us about this—one is Mark 3:29 and the other is Matthew 12:31.[1] I doubt if any of you has ever been guilty of this tragic and unpardonable sin. But there is always danger. The Pharisees were guilty of this tragic and deadly sin because of their pride, prejudice, bigotry and unforgiving spirit. They betrayed the highest thing that was in them. They grieved, and then finally blasphemed, the Holy Ghost. Jesus said they had not forgiveness.

Another way we treat the Spirit in our time is to resist Him. Resisting the Holy Spirit is chronically disagreeing with God and persistently disobeying the leadings of the Spirit. Disobedience has become the sin that we shrug off. Someone will say in testimony, "I love the Lord. He is good to me, and He is patient with me," and then they will say, "I disobey Him; I admit it, I disobey Him." It was disobedience that wrought the fall. One act of disobedience plunged us into this moral mess we are in now. Disobedience is not a light sin to be shrugged off.

If you looked me in the face and said, "Mr. Tozer, I have just been to a doctor. I have cancer," you would not chuckle and shrug and say, "I am all right; I only have cancer." Chronic disobedience breeds cancer of the soul.

Instead of resisting God, resisting what you know is true, resisting the findings of your own conscience as enlightened in the Word and resisting the instructions of the Book, I recommend you cease to chortle over that which brought the fall of man, made a devil out of a cherub and brings grief to the Holy Ghost. If we persistently oppose His leadings, as known from the Bible which the Holy Spirit wrote and as felt in our own hearts by the indwelling presence of the Holy Spirit, we are grieving the Holy Ghost.

The very fact that He can grieve proves that He loves. The psychological nature of grief is such that it cannot be felt where there is not love. A father goes to the police court and there he sees two boys. They have been caught red-handed in some terrible crime. One of them is his own lad who grew up in his home, and the other is a perfect stranger for whom he has no feeling at all. For one boy he may have a sort of pity, but for the other boy he has bitter grief, because grief can only be felt where there is love, and love breeds grief when the object of our love displeases us and offers us affront. So the very fact that the Holy Ghost can grieve is the proof that He is the Spirit of love.

He is not an angry Holy Spirit nor a flippant Holy Spirit. There is so much flippancy among Christians these days. The evangelist tells a story, and he always sets it up so there is a punch line— he, of course, is the hero of the punch line. Everybody laughs and it sounds all right, but that is flippancy.

But the Holy Spirit never deals frivolously with anything. He deals with loving seriousness, but He is never heavy. Heaviness comes from our flesh, or something we ate, or from the bad air in a building, or whatever it might be, but the Holy Ghost always has a sprightliness (if I may so express it), a moral sprightliness. He has about Him something of the song of the birds and the beauty of the sunshine, the loveliness of the landscape and the freshness of the baby's voice. He has about Him all the freshness, creativeness and the beauty of God's primal creation for He made it.

God the Great Musician

The Holy Ghost is always fresh, original and loving, yet He is always serious. Heavy-heartedness and long-facedness are never borne of the Holy Ghost, for the Holy Ghost is mirthful, and it is written in the Old Testament that God sings over His children. He sings over them and rejoices over them. It is written that in the creation the morning stars sang together (Job 38:7).

The old Greeks used to talk about "the music of the spheres." They conceived the idea that the heavenly bodies gave off music as they moved. I do not know whether they do or not, but I think it would be quite expected that they would. God Almighty is the musician of the universe, the great song leader of the world, who dances through His universe like the beat of a baton, who brings music wherever there is anything created, who put the chortle in the throat of the baby and the song in the throat of the thrush, and who gave us hymnody and all the music of the world. God sings over His people.

If you will listen in your heart, you may hear God rejoicing in His family. A father comes home at night tired, but not too tired to sit down and take a baby or two on his lap and talk with them, maybe even break out into a song. I sang our first baby to sleep the first year of his life, and I do not know how he ever survived, but he is thirty-two years old now and several inches taller than I, so God must have translated my bad baritone into sweet music to my boy. It is perfectly normal for a father to sing over his family. So God sings and the Holy Ghost is the Spirit of Love and of music and of sweetness.

He is here, and He is not angry or heavy-browed, but He is serious, and He is loving, and He is grieved when we resist Him we quench Him by dimming His light and putting it out—damping the fire of His of enthusiasm within our heart out of fear. He wants us to testify, and we don't. He wants us to pray, and we have got something else to do. He wants us to go to a friend and talk quietly about Jesus to him, and we are too busy or scared—plain scared. We quench the Holy Ghost. According to the text, all those things grieve Him. But this is for Christians only. The world cannot grieve the Holy Ghost, I suppose, in the sense a Christian can.

The Hidden God

What are the consequences of a grieved Spirit? He hides Himself. "Thou art a God that hidest thyself, O God of Israel" (Isaiah 45:15). God hidden is the Church's woe; God revealed is the Church's glory.

What is a revival but a sudden revelation of God in the hearts of people? Now the preparation for that revival is something else again, but the revival itself is nothing more than a sudden flashing in of the consciousness of "Why, God was here all the time! And my God in whom I live is now pressing in upon me like the air seeking to enter my heart." We throw our heart open and say, "Come, blessed Holy Ghost." That is revival, but this is the age of a grieved Holy Spirit. I do not hesitate to say it.

I have not long to go before I will meet my Savior, and I cannot afford to fool around, so I want to say frankly that I could be extreme in my position. There may be churches, schools, colleges and groups here and there that are better than I know, but I have been around quite a little, and I think I can say that almost universally the Spirit of God is being quenched within His Church. He has not forsaken us. I do not believe in that. But He is grieved within us.

If you hurt the feelings of a friend, he doesn't leave you, but he talks to you with an obvious chilliness upon his heart. He is not angry; He is hurt. The Holy Ghost is like that. He does not leave, but He tightens up. He ceases to be free, homelike with us. He wants to be like a member of the family, but we grieve Him by resisting Him and quenching Him by our habits.

The Holy Ghost suggests in Ephesians 4:31 how we can grieve Him. He mentions bitterness, anger, clamor, evil-speaking and malice. He also mentions in Ephesians 5:3-4 fornication, uncleanness, covetousness, filthiness, foolish talking, improper jesting; those things which the Holy Ghost says in a blessed understatement (in our English)—"are not convenient." Certainly they are not convenient. These are the things that hinder revival.

I am convinced there is not a college student body in the world—in spite of all the hard work and study, burning the midnight oil and hurrying to make classes and all the rest—that could not have a glorious, high-level, sweet revival all the time. And I am sure there is not a church in the whole world that could not have maintained within it a beautiful, high-level, joyous revival all the time—if we would get honest with ourselves and deal with the things that grieve the Holy Spirit.

Bitterness, wrath, uncleanness, impurity, dishonesty, cheating, failing to pay our bills, complaining, lying, excessive exaggeration, levity and frivolity—these things grieve the Holy Ghost and keep Him from working. You may have been praying for a long time for your pal, and he is not saved yet. Maybe he could be, but he has not seen in you that which makes him want what you have. A grieved Holy Ghost keeps the light out of your countenance.

Let us be serious. Let us cut everything else to the bone, and let us deal with our relation to this Person who is in our midst.

[This sermon was delivered at Wheaton College, Pierce Chapel, September 30, 1952.]

CHAPTER

4

The Enemy Within

T o speak of the essence of sin, we must begin
with God; otherwise we will not know what
we mean. From the book of Exodus, the third
chapter, I break into a wonderful story at verse 10.
"Come now therefore," God is saying to Moses,

> and I will send thee unto Pharaoh, that thou
> mayest bring forth my people the children of
> Israel out of Egypt.
>
> And Moses said unto God, Who am I, that
> I should go unto Pharaoh, and that I should
> bring forth the children of Israel out of
> Egypt? And he said, Certainly I will be with
> thee; and this shall be a token unto thee, that
> I have sent thee: When thou has brought
> forth the people out of Egypt, ye shall serve
> God upon this mountain. And Moses said
> unto God, Behold, when I come unto the
> children of Israel, and shall say unto them,
> The God of your fathers hath sent me unto
> you; and they shall say to me, What is his
> name? what shall I say unto them? And God
> said unto Moses, I AM THAT I AM: and he

said, Thus shalt thou say unto the children
of Israel, I AM hath sent me unto you. (3:10-
14)

Certainly there is nothing of greater impor-
tance than the one behind all the phenomena
that we know as nature, behind all mind, spirit,
matter, motion and law: God. This one word
gives meaning to life. If you were to rule out of
human thought the word God and all that clus-
ters around that word, you would not have any
valid reason at all for existence; nobody could
show why we ought to live. As soon as we intro-
duce the word God, then we have a reason for
existence. God is the foundation and the source
of all there is. God is to the universe what our
blood is to our bodies, and what our souls are to
our bodies.

Many years ago in England, there once gathered
together a number of the great Christian leaders of
a certain Protestant group who were attempting to
formulate a creed, or articles of faith. They all
agreed and did all right on most of it, but they had
one word that they could not define or get any
proper description for: *God.*

They got into an impasse; no one seemed to be
able to do it for reasons that are obvious to the
humblest of us. Then in order to break the dead-
lock and somehow get some light on it, the mod-
erator said to a young preacher sitting off to the
side, "Will you lead us in prayer? Let us pray once
more for the light of God on this."

And he got up and clutched the seat in front of him and prayed, "Oh, God, Thou art a Spirit, infinite, eternal, unchangeable in Thy being, wisdom, power, holiness, justice, goodness and truth," and someone cried out, "That's it! That's it!" and they took it down. Ever since that we have had the famous expression, "God is a Spirit, infinite, eternal, unchangeable in His being, wisdom, power, holiness, justice, goodness and truth"—*I AM THAT I AM.*

It was an archbishop who once said,

> over all things and under all things and outside all things:
> > within, but not enclosed;
> > without, but not excluded;
> > above, but not raised up;
> > below, but not depressed;
> > wholly above presiding,
> > wholly beneath sustaining,
> > wholly without embracing
> > and wholly within filling.

It was one man's conception of God. I have often quoted it and often walked around thinking about it, for it embraces so much that God is trying to say to us about Himself. Another old Latin father said this about God:

> At the contemplation of God's majesty all eloquence is dumb, for God is always greater than anything that can be said about Him, and no language is worthy of Him. He is

more sublime than all sublimity and loftier than all loftiness and profounder than all profundity, more splendid than all splendor and more powerful than all power, more majestic than all majesty, and more merciful than all mercy.

These men were simply trying to say what the Bible says all the time about God, that God *is*.

Moses knew that if he was going to go down into Egypt he would have to be sent. Moses said unto God, "Behold, when I come unto the children of Israel, and shall say unto them, the God of your fathers hath sent me unto you; and they shall say to me 'What is His name?' What shall I say unto them?" And God said, "You go tell them that I AM sent you. I AM THAT I AM."

That is the sacred word, the Tetragrammaton, the incommunicable name, the name that is covered up in the King James Version by the capital letters for Lord. The old translators felt that it was too holy to use carelessly or even unnecessarily, so they shielded it under the word LORD in places. To this day, they say that in the Near East if a person who cannot read sees a piece of paper lying on the floor, he or she will pick it up and reverently keep it high and say, "Perhaps the name of God may be on that." No one would want to be guilty of inadvertently trampling the name of God down into the dust.

God is Self-existent Selfhood—that's what He means here. You will excuse me, I hope, for attempting to explain that which is beyond any man, but we are trying to blunder into it the best we can and hoping that God will save the pieces. Here, out of the expression *I AM THAT I AM*, we have stated Self-existing Selfhood.

"God has no origin," said one of the church fathers. The very word "origin" is a creature word and it means and testifies whether it is willed or not. It is applied to everything that has breath or has existence because it indicates that it started somewhere, originated somewhere. It is the one word that cannot be used for God. God has no origin; He is the Creator.

When we use the word "origin," it testifies that all things that exist are dependent, that they are relative, that they came out of something, that they are a reflection of some original, that they are water out of some ancient fountain, that they do not exist in themselves, that they cannot stand up in their own might, but that they flow from some invisible source.

One time a gentleman wrote me a nice but very sharp letter, with a word of rebuke because I had said something nice about Joseph Addison. He said, "Don't you know that Joseph Addison belonged to the school of seventeenth-century rationalists? And all he could say about God was that the mighty heavens above and all the sweep of the galaxy testify of their Great Original. The very word 'original' brands him as being a rationalist. He is not a Christian at all."

I have no trouble with the term "Great Original"—none whatsoever in the wide world. Addison tells us that the sun and the moon and the stars shout that the hand that made them is divine. They can label Addison as they will; I still can use the words the "Great Original" in capital letters for that is exactly what God is. He is the original for which there is no origin. He has given meaning and life and existence to all things that be. This God, the original Self, *I AM THAT I AM*, underived, uncreated eternal self, is God.

Let us look at the word "self." It went for a walk one night with a man named Adam, and it got in bad company, so the word "self" is a bad word now in theological circles, as well it ought to be. Somebody said, "Turn it around, tack an 'h' on it, and you have 'flesh.' " That is true also, but God is the originating Self out of which all other selves originate, and there is nothing sinful there. God is that Holy Being, unsupported, independent and Self-existent.

I preached a sermon one time in which I said that God did not need us. It bothered some people because they felt that that was carrying it just a little bit too far; they always felt somehow, even though they were good believers, that God did secretly feel that if we ran out on Him, His world would collapse. I never did think that, and I do not think it now. My brethren, God does not need you, and God does not need a broad-winged angel by the throne of light. God does not need any creature.

The poet said that "creation has not set Thee on a higher throne." Only God's heart needs us. God in His uncreated Being does not need us; He was before there was anything, and if it were all to be beaten back out of existence, into ancient nothingness, God would still be the same God forever and ever, unperturbed, world without end. But God's heart needs us.

Let me bring it down a bit from the stratosphere and illustrate it like this: There is a man who is a very rich house-holder. He has three cars, two garages, life insurance and everything that an American businessman is supposed to have. He has a fine wife who thinks he is the only man in the world. He is accepted every place socially, belongs to the country club and plays golf. In fact, his golf balls would not even look at ordinary golf balls. He is way up there and does not need anybody at all; he is self-sufficient.

But do you know what he has not got? He has not got a baby around the place, and his poor, hungry heart cannot live on golf balls and bank accounts. Financially, he does not need any children around the place; he does not need anything. But as he walks around trying to look tough, in that sissy heart of his there is a longing to hold a baby in his arms. He does not need the baby, but his heart needs the baby.

So when one comes into the home, the woman gets the credit for loving the baby, but the man is the one who really goes crazy about the infant. That is because the man has a heart in him, and I say God gave him that heart, the God of the Great Original, and the heart of man came from the heart of God.

God does not need anybody, for He is the unsupported, independent, self-existent God. Self in
God is no sin. A great English poet named Faber,[1]
one of the greatest God-lovers since Augustine,
dared this line: he said that God admired Himself
and loved Himself, without sin. I would cautiously
use such an expression, but the poet had liberty
and license, and he did not go too far. It is proper
and right to say that God loves Himself because all
love flows out of God and back into Him again,
and the love of God for Himself is the holiest thing
that archangels can dream of.

The old theologians used to say there has to be
three Persons in the Trinity because God the Father is love, and He loves God the Son with all the
uncreated love of His Fatherhood, but there has to
be a means of communication between the Father
and the Son, equal to both so that the outpoured
love of the Father might be received without being
diminished by the Son, and that which linked the
Father and the Son is the Holy Ghost. Thus, they
argue for the Trinity.

I do not know that their argument is waterproof.
I do not know that if I did not believe in the Trinity that I would accept it because of that argument—but I think it is a delightful argument
anyway. I believe that God loves Himself, and the
Persons love each other and honor each other because God is the uncreated Self in whom there is
no sin and could not sin because He is God.

What is sin then? When a creature made by God
with moral perception, conscience, the knowledge

of right and wrong, an ego and a relative, essential self, goes into rebellion against God and says, "I will arise"—there is the essence of sin. The first sin in the Bible is not the sin of Eve. It went way back to the very storms of fire by the throne of God when a created being dared to exalt his contingent and relevant self against the great uncreated Self we call God. He dared to defy God through his teeth and say, "I will arise." The essence of all sin is the rebellion of the creature against the Creator.

Sin has many symptoms and many manifestations. There are sins of the mind, will, affections, flesh, but they all flow out of the liquid essence of the bottle containing the poisonous essence called self: self-will, self-love, self-confidence, self-everything. There is nothing wrong with self. God made me a self and He distinguished me from my brother who is also a self. But God, who spells his SELF in capital letters, spells my name in lower-case letters. God, who puts my self in Roman letters, puts His own *SELF* in italics.

The God who had no origin made me. I had an origin; I come like the sunbeam from the sun. If a sunbeam coming down from the sun at the speed of 186,000 miles a second were suddenly to go into rebellion—if such a thing were possible—and say, "I will not look to the sun anymore; I am on my own," he would cut himself off from the central sun, cease to be and plunge into everlasting darkness.

That is exactly what happened to the human

race. We are all here, and we are all in one piece, and we have the self that God gave us, but we have cruelly and sinfully wrenched ourselves loose from the originating Self, God the Father Almighty, Maker of heaven and earth, as it says so sweetly in the creeds. We have said to God, "I will arise."

One text in the Bible that sums up all that I could say or think on this subject, Isaiah 53:6, reads, " . . . we have turned every one to his own way." That was Isaiah's description of the sinner for whom Jesus had to die in love. The difference between Christ and the antichrist is that Jesus said, "Thy will be done," and the antichrist says, "My will be done." The difference between the highest saint and the sinner is, "Not my will but thine," and "my will, my will." The essence of all sin is setting up my stubborn will against the will of God.

Sometimes in our evangelistic meetings, particularly in young people's meetings, we unintentionally degrade this. We act as though we could accept Jesus as our Savior and not accept Him as our Lord—as though we could divorce His Saviourhood from His Lordship. I have heard men say, "Just accept Jesus, that is all you have to do, and it is all right with you; you will go right to heaven zooming through like jet propulsion! Just accept Jesus; take this gospel and go." So we send them out confused, bewildered and wholly without any proper concept of what the gospel really means.

Jesus Christ is not two, but one, and He cannot save whom He cannot control. His office cannot be separated. If you will not have Him as your Lord then you do not have Him as your Savior, and you are self-deceived. We tell them, "Come on, now, maybe in fifteen or twenty years you can take Him as your Lord and maybe go to China." No! It is all wrong!

I believe that Jesus Christ is one. All His glorious offices are indivisible. If I take Him, I take all of Him, and He will not save me if He cannot boss me. He will not deliver me from hell if He cannot deliver me from self. Self is the essence of sin.

The text says, "We have turned every one to his own way." This is a lovely, poetic description of this devilish rebellion of the human heart against God. We have turned, everybody, to our own way. The ways are not all the same. They are as many as there are people, but we have turned to our own way. It is not the way we have turned to but the fact that it is our own way that curses us and puts the blight upon us forever.

We were not created to have our own way. We were created to stand and gaze at God in delight and obey Him like the creatures that Ezekiel saw (Ezekiel 1), finding all our delight in doing His holy will. One of these days God is all you are going to have. Today you have other things— your ambitions and your great dreams. I used to dream when I was in my middle teens that I was going to do great deeds some day—be known around the world and all that. How I thank God that I have been delivered from such delusions, dreams of youth. But if you should gain all that you dream and plan, it will turn out to be the way of despair, loss and woe. But the way of God—oh, what a gentle way!

Heinrich Sousa, the famous German devotional man of generations ago, said, "God does not want to keep you from pleasure; He wants to give you all pleasure, which is Himself." God wants to deliver us from selfish pleasure that we might have selfless pleasure forever.

Self-will is the great sin, for it is rebellion against the Lord of Creation. It is an insult to royalty and, in essence, a lethal sin. There is the woe that lies upon the proud, untrusting, self-centered and self-preserving. We forget that Jesus said, "Except a corn of wheat fall into the ground and die, it abideth alone" (John 12:24), and we try to preserve ourselves by self-feeding, self-loving, self-defending. "Oh, to be saved from myself, dear Lord, Oh, to be lost in Thee."[2]

That stubborn will is your trouble. You say, "My trouble, Mr. Tozer, is that my temper gets in the way." No—that is bad enough, God knows, but that is not the essence of it. The root of your trouble is that *you* are still in control of things. Your trouble is not impurity nor dishonesty, and those are sins that fill the cup and bring the wrath of God, but at the root of all these sins of the mind and flesh is that central, ancient rebellion of the spirit of man against God. The essence of sin is rebellion.

When we preach consecration, when we preach that we ought to lay ourselves at the cross of Jesus and die there with Him that we might rise to newness of life (Romans 6:4), we are not preaching a fancy Christianity. We are preaching the only Christianity the New Testament contains. He that would save his self shall lose it, and he that will lose it for His sake shall keep it unto everlasting life (see Matthew 16:25). Here is the eternal wisdom of Paul's statement, "Not I, but Christ" (Galatians 2:20).

Do you ever feel so good you do not know what to do with yourself? The old writers used to call that "animal spirits." You can live on that. You can live on ambitions and hopes. You can live on service Christianity: you can teach, sing, play the Jew's harp and be soloist in the choir back at home. You can do lots of things and still not actually know what it means ever to have a cross like a sword go into your heart to slay the old rebellious self, to rise again in newness of life free from its curse, to follow Jesus and run the race set before you without hindrance and without the weights that you carry (Hebrews 12:1).

When you are by yourself, stop and check up on yourself and try to get in touch with God about all this. Are you examining your life? I would like to make it easier, but I cannot. If I made it easier I would be a liar and betrayer. Self is your trouble. Take up your cross and deny yourself (Luke 9:23).

I do not mean to deny your homeland and go to Africa, or to deny some big paying job and become a pastor—that is not it. It is profounder, more essential and more basic than that. Jehovah's Witnesses do that. Soldiers leave America and go to Korea. Do you think you deserve a crown as big as a washtub because you are willing to leave a job here in the United States and go to China? Business people do that. That is not necessarily noble.

There is a self that is deeper than all that, and it must die or it will keep you down. Do you want to be saved from yourself, that unreconstructed rebel within your spirit, that stubborn self-will that flings your head and says, "I will"? Do you want to be saved from it? I only know one way. You cannot discipline it out of you; that will help but will not kill it. You cannot educate it out of you; that will refine you but it will not kill self. Only the cross of Jesus can slay the enemy within my breast.

> Oh cross, that lifteth up my head,
> I dare not ask to hide from thee;
> I lay in dust, life's glory dead,
> And from the ground there blossoms red,
> Life that shall endless be.[3]

[This sermon was delivered at Wheaton College, Pierce Chapel, September 30, 1952.]

CHAPTER

5

Wounds from God

Faithful are the wounds of a friend; but the kisses of an enemy are deceitful. (Proverbs 27:6)

I want to talk to you about the faithful wounds of God. I have been thinking about a woman who lived 600 years ago and what she said about wounds. She lived before Luther's time and of course never heard of the Protestants. Nevertheless, I am sure that if she had ever met Luther she would have come out wholeheartedly on the side of the evangelicals, because she was evangelical, born out of due time.

She was an Englishwoman and has only written, so far as I know, one book, and it is so small that you could tuck it into your pocket and hardly have a bulge. It is called *Revelations of Divine Love*. I speak, of course, of Lady Julian.

Lady Julian was a Spirit-enlightened woman who met God without very much light and put to shame the people of today who have lots of light and fail to meet Him often. She met Him; God revealed His truth to her; and in this little book she made a great deal of God. God was her all in all—

63

the Blissful Trinity, as she called God. She made a great deal of man's terrible sin, and particularly her terrible sin.

She also emphasized with great joy what she called the making of amends through Jesus' dreadful suffering. She brought the atonement before our gaze and held it in full focus until we could weep for the joy of knowing that though we had sinned so against the Blissful Trinity, one of that Trinity had come and in His hard suffering on the cross had canceled out all our demerit. Jesus Christ made us acceptable to God so that we could be what she called in her archaic English, "one with God," that is, united with God.

This little lady lived a pretty cloistered life and probably never heard of the movements and motions and currents of spiritual revival that were moving even then in England and through Europe which finally culminated in the revival, or the Reformation as we call it, under Martin Luther. Nevertheless, she was a part of the Reformation long before it was ever born; she was herself a Roman Catholic, but she was a happy Catholic.

In her book she never talks about Mary except to say that God was awfully good to Mary in letting her be the mother of her Lord. She said something to the effect that it was all right to pray according to their set forms, but she knew a better way—just talk to God through Jesus Christ the Lord, and she did it and practiced it for a lifetime.

She was a very happy lady—she lived a very

happy life and she gave out sunshine and spiritual radiation to everybody around her. She would have been at home among the Methodists, even though Wesley was not born for hundreds of years after that. But one time she said she got to thinking about how high and lofty Jesus was and yet how He made Himself so meek and lowly as to commune with her and she said, "The delight of it swept over my soul 'til I shouted out loud, 'Praise the Lord!' " Then she apologized and said she did not know just quite why "me did it." For, you know, it was not quite proper for a staid English lady to let go like that, but it was too big for her, the wonder of it.

Lady Julian lived and died like that, and I certainly expect to see her in heaven when I get there. In the early part of her life she prayed to God for three things. She said, "I conceived a mighty desire to receive three wounds in my life," and she named them. She said, "I want the wound of very contrition, the wound of kind compassion and the wound of earnest longing after God."

The Wound of Contrition

First was the wound of very contrition. Her whole concept of sin was so pointed, so sharp, so painful to her that she was afraid to take the goodness of God without allowing the grief of sin to do its healing work in her heart. She prayed that she might never get so far up that she would forget that she had been a sinner and that sin had wounded the second Person of the Blessed Trinity. She begged God to let her feel the sharp sword of sin.

A great Danish preacher [Soren Kierkegaard][1] whom I do not follow in everything, but who says many good things, complained in one of his great sermons about what he calls the light and superficial quality of repentance. He says that often we mistake moral impatience for repentance. We are mad at ourselves. We sin, and we are angry with ourselves because we had better hope for ourselves. He says we mistake anger with ourselves for true repentance. Then he goes on to say that a true Christian will be known by the depth of his repentance. Wherever you find a true Christian man or woman—whatever their denomination—they will be known for the depth and sincerity of their repentance.

No man could believe in the grace of God more than I, nor contain any more joy for the grace of God than I. But while the grace of God redeems and salvation is by grace, I am not going to allow myself to forget while I live in this world that I have sinned against the Triune God. I want that thing to sting me sometimes, particularly if I raise my head a little bit or tend to boast a little.

I believe this healing wound is good for the soul. Lady Julian prayed, "God, wound me with very contrition. Make me sorry that I ever sinned, and keep me there." Though Paul was so joyous that he could write Philippians, the joy epistle, from a prison, throughout his epistles there will recur occasionally indications that Paul had never quite forgotten what a sinner he had been.

I do not believe we will ever have the expected

revival in America until we have again a generation of prophets that shall rise up and deal with
sin. I will not preach against bobbed hair and lip-
stick, the little incidental sins which may or may
not be bad, but I will deal with sin as it relates to
the holy Trinity, and make us feel again what our
Calvinistic forebears made us feel until we
crawled on our knees with it. The exceeding sin-
fulness of sin (Romans 7:13), because it was an act
done against the exceedingly holy God, is wound
number one—the wound of very contrition.

The Wound of Compassion

The second is the wound of kind compassion.
Lady Julian wanted to suffer with Jesus and feel as
He felt about the world and grieve with the world.
I think that is the greatest hindrance to Christianity today—not modernism, nor communism, but
un-Christlike Christians. These people display a
hard orthodoxy that has never felt compassion. Instead they ram a crumpled tract into the fist of the
sinner and make him take it. They push John 3:16
down his throat with a ramrod, look him in the
eye and make him feel that he is an uncircumcised
Philistine while they pretend to be God's chosen
people.

A hard Christianity never could have won me.
My father was a high-tempered, blazing English-
man and there is too much of that in me to ever
be won by one of these mean-looking, cocky
soul-winners that read the book *How to Win*

Souls in Seven Easy Lessons. I would have turned my back on him, and though I only weigh 160 pounds, I think I would have probably bowled him over. I never could take religion without compassion. To me, it is a skeleton without meat and without life.

I worry a little about myself (probably more than I should) because I do not love people more. Some people just spill all over you—their eyes are always wet and they have a handkerchief handy continually because they just love you so much, but sometimes they weigh me down. There used to be a fellow I knew who always wanted to grab me and kiss me, and the trouble was he always had two days' growth of beard, and I did not react well to that! I am not talking about that slobbery kind of compassion.

I wonder and worry because I have not loved more. But God is comforting my heart a little because He is showing me that compassion is love, of a sort. It is another side of love. I do not know that I love people so tremendously but I pity people until I grieve in the night season.

I pity the lad who has to go to Korea.[2] I pity the boy who lies over there face up, not seeing the stars. I pity the poor mother who is left here at home. I pity the little fellow who plays on Wednesday, gets a sore throat on Thursday and on Friday is crippled for life with polio. I pity people until I am in misery most of the time, or at least a good part of the time. This is the kind of wound that God has most graciously given me in my heart, a wound I never want to heal. I want to feel with people—compassion, suffering and co-suffering. I want to be able to suffer along with other people.

This is closest to my heart and the thing I feel that we need the most in this awful hour—compassion. I have a little prayer book here which I got in the ten-cent store. It was blank when I bought it, and I have written my own prayers into it and have carried it around for years. One of my prayers is, "Oh, Lord Jesus, help me to feel exactly as you feel about people. Help me to love them exactly as you love them and in the same way that you love them." God may be answering that prayer a little by letting me suffer compassion for the woes of the world.

I am afraid that even some of our soul-winning is little more than zeal to make proselytes, but there must be tears along with it. Moody is quoted as saying a lot of things he never said, but Moody is quoted as having said that no man had the right to preach on hell except he preach with tears in his eyes.[3] He loved them and pitied them, and so this love and pity, down through the years, has been a stream of gospel sincerity; it has been the evidence of the indwelling Jesus who wept over Jerusalem and who went out to die.

The wound of compassion is a faithful wound, my friend, and I ask that you seriously think about this with me and when you can, pray to God about it. Let your prayer be, "Oh God, give me and keep in my heart the wound of very compassion and the wound of very contrition. Let me feel how bad

I have been, but also, let me feel how terribly dis-
tressful the world is, and let me suffer along with
the poor suffering world."

The Wound of Longing after God

Last, there is the wound of an earnest longing after God, as Lady Julian called it. I do not want to
go maudlin on you here. I am not one ever to in-
troduce the romantic sex-relationship, that we call
"falling in love," because sometimes I just get em-
barrassed when I hear evangelists getting too intimate. It is proper to stay within the bounds of
Scripture when I say that love is a kind of wound.

When you are forced to read the old English poetry, you will find a great many of those old boys
celebrated the wound they had, carrying around a
broken heart because the lady to whom they wrote
the sonnet was busy looking after somebody else.
Nowadays they moo; they stick their head over a
fence and bellow over a pair of hard tonsils. Usually they rhyme moon with soon and so on. It is
not so graceful, but it is the same old wound.

I have seen men and women come to me
wounded, hurt as though they had been stabbed,
bleeding at their heart, further than their physical
heart because they had been disappointed and de-
ceived. I have had them come to me when they
could not cry anymore; they had cried until there
were no more tears. Their very longing was never
satisfied because someone upon whom they had
set all their hopes had disappointed them.

My friends, there is such a thing as longing after God that is bigger than anything else in life. David talked about it, and Paul told about it. He said, "I do not consider myself yet to have attained but I press forward" (Philippians 3:13-14, author's paraphrase). We see Paul in the home stretch, like a runner, straining forward to win the prize. And the prize, to Paul, was God. Paul was never satisfied until the Roman sword severed his head from his shoulders. Never? Maybe when he wrote Second Timothy God had brought him satisfaction at last, but it was not long afterward that he was beheaded.

Lady Julian said, "Give me thyself, for Thou art enough to me. And if I ever ask anything less than that, why I ever will be wanting, but only in Thee I have all." The quaint English makes it sweeter still—"Thou art enough to me," she said. And so she prayed, "Oh, God, wound me and keep me always homesick."

Ray McAfee said to me that fourteen years ago he appeared here, greener than lettuce, on these grounds. He said, "I set my suitcase down in the middle of the floor and prayed that I could die. I was the most homesick boy in the whole wide world."

They say that American soldiers are the most homesick boys of all the soldiers known any place. All other soldiers manage somehow to toughen up and take it, but they say Americans are just homesick to the point where they do not care. I was in the First World War, that is, I was in the service, but I never got into combat. After it was over and we knew we were going home but did not know when, one of the fellows working there with me used to sing "Home, Sweet Home." I thought it was a joke, but it was not—the fellow was so homesick he did not care if they laughed at him. He sang "Home, Sweet Home" off key until he was released.

Homesickness is the longing for the old familiar streets and the old signs, the friendly dog that you know, the familiar creaky steps and all that you have come to associate with the people you love. Longing can be a disease. It is not wrong when we call it homesickness, for it certainly is that. This woman prayed, "Oh, God, wound me with an incurable homesickness, so that I will never settle down in this world and feel at home here."

Never feel at home. I do not care for many Negro spirituals—I think white people have spoiled the music—but there is one Negro spiritual I like to hear sometimes. That one says, "I cannot feel at home in this world anymore." That is what I meant—I just cannot feel at home anymore in this world. The whole center of things has been shifted to another world from this.

You say, "That is fine for an old fellow who has lost half his hair and the other half is turned gray, but what about me? Here I am young, full of zing and all the rest—what about me?" Anything God can do for an old man, God can do for a young man or a young woman. Don't think age makes you spiritual; age simply may make you intolerable, and it often does.

I know what George Mueller[4] meant when he prayed, "Oh, God, do not let me live to be a wicked old man." I have found people who knew God in their youth, and are still Christians because their names are written yonder. They are God's children but they are terribly hard to live around; they are nasty Christians. Thank God for justification and imputed human righteousness because that is the only hope those boys will ever have.

Clothed in His righteousness alone,
Faultless to stand before the throne.

They will stand before the throne, but nobody wants to stand around them here very much because growing age and increasing years has not sweetened but soured them. They are critical of everybody and everything; they forget they were ever born; they thought they were fifty years old when their mothers brought them forth. They forget the mighty throbbings, yearnings and dreams that belong to youth.

Age does not make you holy; God makes you holy through Jesus Christ, the blood of the Lamb and the indwelling Spirit. Anything that Lady Julian can have, you can have. She was thirty-two, incidentally, when she prayed this famous prayer which God answered and made her a core of sweet spiritual energy. I am not sure but what it was such as she, one hidden here and one hidden there, that gave Luther and the rest the groundwork which later eventuated the Reformation.

The rest of her prayer ran like this: "Oh, God, all this I ask without any condition whatsoever." Do you see what I mean? She prayed, "Oh, God, ner I have been. Even when I am rejoicing with such delight that I cannot keep from shouting, 'Glory to God!' I will yet remember in the back of my heart that I have been a sinner.

"And then wound me, God, with compassion so that I can suffer with all the poor sinful world, so my religion will never be service that I take for granted, never be so joyful that the devils are subjected unto me and I forget that the poor, suffering, bleeding, heartbroken world walking in the twilight with no place to look, no hope of a sunrise, needs my compassion.

"And then, Oh God, wound me with love for Thyself until it becomes an incurable homesickness, 'til I thirst for Thee and spend all my life cultivating God, and this I ask without condition."

She prayed without condition. "Do these things for me and do not pay any attention to what it costs, for my will is Thine; I will take the cross, bear it on my shoulders and pay the price you enable me here on earth, but give me these three wounds."

"Faithful are the wounds of a friend" (Proverbs 27:6). The world will kiss you and then betray you, the flesh will fondle you and then betray you, but the faithful God will wound you deep and then heal you as deep as He wounds you. He will cleanse, purge, purify and make you "one with God," as the old lady said. Is that not what your heart longs for?

[This sermon was delivered at Wheaton College, Pierce Chapel, date unknown.]

Five Keys to the Faithful Christian Life

The talk I want to give tonight is one I almost gave before. I was at Winona[1] last summer at the conference there, and I mentioned this at the conclusion of a sermon that I had preached on something else. A WMBI[2] brother over there asked me whether I would give it on the radio. With some changes, I am going to give it tonight. This definitely will not be a sermon. I am going to do a Nixon on you tonight and just let down my hair, figuratively speaking, and talk to you out of my heart about something that is very real and very precious to me.[3]

I hope that you will not be disappointed but rather you will be pleased because I have respected your right to make your own decisions and have not given you a welter of deathbed stories; neither have I stamped you with any evangelistic high-pressured methods. Instead, I have given the Word as I know it and then have allowed you to make up your own mind. That is the only thing I believe in.

I admit that I have an Irish streak that gets in me from somewhere, but I do not want to entertain you; I want to help you, and I am assuming that you are serious-minded, not gloomy. I have been reading about the saints, and I find that they all have a sense of humor. One authority claims that in the Roman Church the one factor that always has to be present before they will make a person a saint is that it has to be proved that he has a sense of humor. They will not canonize long-faced saints.

But serious-mindedness is one thing; gloom is another. God is not gloomy, but He is serious. The church of Jesus is not a gloomy place, but it is a serious place, or it ought to be. So I am assuming tonight that you are serious-minded and then I am also assuming that you have been regenerated. I have not preached on regeneration because I have assumed that you are regenerated.

Maybe you are not. Some of you may have gotten through the screen, and you only *thought* you were regenerated. You accepted Jesus somewhere in a kind of sickly way and got a tract and your name on something and here you are, but you are not sure of yourself, and I would have to give some other message to you. But tonight I am assuming that you are regenerated, and this is for regenerated people—though there would be no reason why hungry-hearted people who are not yet regenerated might not get something out of it.

Assuming that we are regenerated people, that we have been renewed by a crisis—we did not ooze into it or leap into it or grow into it, but we hit a crisis and had a specific, identifiable encounter with the Almighty God at the cross and got up different—assuming that, then the next thing you will want to know is, now what from here? Must I simply grab a handle somewhere and begin to turn, grinding out my religious activities and waiting for the grand climax—or is there something for me better than I know?

Is there a full satisfaction in the gospel system? Can I have inward liberty, outward victory, a reasonable degree of delight and a mystic and numinous sense of the presence of another world? Can I live like that, or must I settle down simply to live it out and grit my teeth? As one dear old lady said, she had learned to grin and bear it—that was all the testimony she had.

A lot of Christians, from the looks on their faces, are just grinning and bearing it. They believe in walking by faith, and faith to them is a grim and bitter affair. But is there something better? I think there is. I believe that there is a better place for us within the framework of fundamental Christianity as you and I know it in the world, and we do not have to import it from somewhere, nor change our views, nor get converted from one "ism" to another. Let us just take what we have and go ahead. I think I can tell you how you can make remarkable and firm progress within a matter of hours, if you want to do it.

I am going to give you five points—the five-point program for spiritual progress.

First of all, could I say that I know what I am talking about here? A few years ago there came to my life a crisis—one that centered around what I have been speaking on tonight. I had been doing all right and getting along all right. Some people were getting helped, or they kindly said they were, but I was not satisfied. And then I came to the place where it was forced upon me by the good, kind hand of God to make some vows and reach a crisis, and I did. Actually only four of these points stood out solidly with me then, but I have prefixed one for the sake of beginners.

If you are going on with God and you are going to leave the dead level of dull Christianity and climb Jacob's ladder and get into the rarefied air where the saints of the ages have lived, then you have got to take some vows. David vowed his vows, and he said he paid them.

Remember, there is a lot about vows in the Old Testament. There is even something about vows in the New Testament. All I mean by vow is that you are going to go before God either here, in your room, out on a bench somewhere under a tree or anywhere you can get quiet and silent to tell God that as far as you are concerned, you are going to do these things. He will have to help you—that is all taken for granted, because there is no good in you. But He believes in vows, and He is going to work along with you in your vows. Here is the first one.

Vow #1: Deal Thoroughly with Sin

You have got to vow to deal with sin thoroughly. We have misunderstood grace in our day. According to some historians, one British preacher so preached grace as to lower the moral standards of the nation. If that is even half true, it is a terrible sentence to so misunderstand the grace of God. Billy Graham said just a little while back, and I so fully agree with him, "It is a strange thing that in this hour there is more talk about religion than any time in American history and the moral standards of the nation are lower than they have ever been before."

It is a strange and confusing paradox that while there are more people talking about religion now than ever, we are in a worse moral mess than we have ever been since the days of Finney. It may have been that we are saved by grace, but we misunderstand that and believe that grace gives us a license to do as we please. I tell you there never could be a greater mistake.

The Bible begins its work in a man's soul (or God begins it, according to the Bible) by repentance. There must be a violent and aggressive repentance in the soul, and that individual, whether he is five years old or fifty, must come to God and repent. I appreciate the fact that a child has not many external sins to repent of, but without some understanding of lostness I do not see how there can be any understanding of salvation. We must deal with it thoroughly.

I do not say you are worse than others, but I do not say you are better. I say we are an average crowd, and I know how ever-present and insidious sin is, how brazen it is, how ubiquitous it is. It is everywhere, pushing and pressing in from all di-

rections. It is all but omnipresent, and it is like trying to walk through a coal mine and come out
clean to walk through this world of ours and keep
our garments clean—and yet it is not an impossibility.

If Jesus Christ is the Savior that He says He is, if
He is the Savior God says He is, and if He is the
Savior that the historic Church says He is, then He
ought to be able to deliver us from the vilest con-
tamination and sin here in this world. You do not
have to believe in eradication to believe in this. I
do not believe that myself; nevertheless, I do believe that there is such a thing as walking in the
Spirit and not fulfilling the lusts of the flesh.

If you are going to go on with God, you are going
to have to start right there with that matter of sin.
God told Israel to drive out all those that dwelled
in the land that had sinned away their right to
live. God said they had forfeited existence. Israel
drove some of them out and let some of them stay,
and the ones they allowed to stay unjudged cursed
them for all their history. The curses of those unholy nations are still upon Israel after the passing
of the centuries.

You are going to have to deal with sin. I have read
bushels of books on psychology and still do not
know any more about it than I did before, but if you
have been fooling around with psychology that excuses sin, reject it. Anything that excuses sin is not of
God and it is not for your welfare. Nowadays if biting
conviction comes on a young soul he rushes off to a
library and reads a book to prove he has got a guilt

complex, or that it was the result of his mother's scolding him when he was three months old, and so the poor fellow goes out feeling that sin is not sin. We have got to deal with the question of sin—it is basic, I say. Grace deals with *sin*, my friends, but grace *deals* with sin. That is point number one.

Vow #2: Do Not Own Anything

Point number two is—and this is going to be harder to understand—we have to vow never to own anything. I will tell you what I mean by that. This came to me at one of the critical moments in my life, and I will never cease to thank God that He wrought this in me. It is not a theory which I have gotten from somewhere, not something I read in an old book or got off a wall motto, but it is a living, burning, blazing reality to my spirit: before God can do much for His children, He's got to detach them from earthly things.

It is not that God does not want you to have things, but He does not want things to have you. It is not that He wants you to go barefoot and beg and live in a cave (as some ancient people did in a poor, misguided effort to be detached from things), but it is that He wants you to have a spiritual crisis that will detach you from things.

I can testify that this is more than a possibility. It can be done. We can arrive at a place in God where we have an understanding with Him, an understanding that is just as valid and just as real as a marriage vow. Just as a young man stands before an altar and says that leaving all others, he takes this one, and it is a vow that remains, so we can go before our God and have an understanding. That young man can then get into the uniform of his country, go around the world and hide himself in some jungle somewhere, but still there is that happy and perfect assurance within him that the marriage vow holds. That is a real vow—a transaction, a crisis.

That happened to me. She is mine, she belongs to me, and though she may be thousands of miles away and though it may be daylight here and night where she is, it does not change the fact that she still wears my ring and still bears my name. That is a crisis in a life, and there can be such a crisis in human life where the mind and the heart and all the mysterious depths of our being can go before the Lord Christ and hand it all over to Him and say, "From now on, Lord, nothing is mine— nothing. My reputation is not mine. I am all nothing—it is all Thine." And God passes His hand all the way around us and cuts all the strings.

We can then drive an automobile with a sweet detachment, knowing that it is God's automobile. We can have a wife or a family with sweet knowledge that the family is not ours, really; it belongs to God. Everything we have we can give to God.

I said during the Second World War (for this crisis came to me before that time) that the only safe place to put a soldier boy was to put him in God's hands. Many a mother imperiled the life of her boy by hanging onto him and tearfully wailing when he had to go.

There is only one way to deal with that which is dear, my brethren, and that is to put the knife in it and let it die. Die with it and rise again, and then God will let you keep it, but it will be so different now. It will not be in you now; it will be outside of you. Instead of being in you to weigh you down and change the direction of your look inward, it will be outside of you now, and you can look upward.

We must get delivered from things. "All my ambitions, plans and wishes at His feet in ashes lay." The woman who wrote that cried herself to sleep over it. I guess she had to give up her poor ambitions. You know what they are? They are treacherous, and they will let you down.

The poet said that he wrote on high a name he deemed would never die, and there is not a boy with good sense and an IQ above twenty-five anywhere in America who has not somewhere or sometime written his name somewhere or dreamed that it would be written and never die. Yet what percentage of people ever get in *Who's Who*? So the thing for you to do is forget that ambition—stop driving and let God drive.

You say, "You want me to relax, sit around, look dumb and never go anywhere or be anything? Is not sanctified ambition a good thing?" You know, when we want to excuse a scoundrel we always put the qualifying adjective "sanctified" ahead of him and then we have got a saint made out of him. We say "sanctified anger," "sanctified ambition" or "sanctified severity," and by using the word "sanctified" we think we canonize wickedness. No, no, my friends, ambition is not for you.

"Seek not these things," God said to Spurgeon out of the Bible (see Luke 12:29-31). Did Charles Spurgeon sit down and look dumb? No, he was one of the greatest preachers of his generation and he is still preaching through his great books to this generation. But God took over. It is useless for you to drive yourself and say, "Now I have got to do this and this and this." Forget it and relax. Get detached and say, "God, I have no ambitions. Show me what you want me to do." And then out of your relaxed, consecrated, quiet heart will come rivers of living water, and God will take over and guide you.

Moses, we say, led the children of Israel through the wilderness. He did no such thing; Moses followed a cloud that was leading him. Moses was detached from things, and you and I must be, so there is point number two. Vow never to own anything and then maybe God will let you own a great deal, but it will be where it should be and will not hurt you.

Vow #3: Do Not Gossip

Then, vow never to pass on a rumor that is injurious to anybody. This may not seem quite important enough to fit in, but I have found it so. I have learned that gossip is a very deadly thing in the Church of Jesus and it certainly can be very injurious to your spiritual life. Let us let John Wesley define evil speaking. He says, "Evil speaking is any unnecessary or uncomplimentary remarks made about anybody."

Sometimes it is necessary to make uncomplimentary remarks about people, if you are a member of a committee or a head of some organization. If people look to you for leadership, then it is necessary sometimes that you tell the truth about a man or woman. But God will bless you graciously if you will vow to let your heart be as silent as the grave when it comes to passing on scurrilous stories about anybody. I will not tell my closest companion on earth outside of my family, Mr. McAfee. I will not tell him evil things I have heard about men. If it comes out and gets around that is something else, but I do not discuss it.

I never tell my wife when I hear that some fellow has gone wrong. I never tell her, never tell Brother McAfee, never whisper it. I keep it in my heart. I will not pass on gossip that is injurious to the character of God's people. That is not my virtue. It is common sense; it is biblical; it is New Testament; it is charity.

We gossip and whisper around about people, and rumors start. Men's futures are wrecked because God's people cannot keep their mouths shut and have not charity enough to just bear it in their hearts. I cannot prevent rumors from traveling, but I will never let them bounce off my empty skull and go on someplace, never while the world stands, so help me God.

If, as a member of a conference, committee or ordaining council I have to sit and pass judgment on the moral fitness of a man for a job, then God will not bless me if I do not do it. That is necessary in the line of duty. Never anything that is not necessary will I pass on.

Vow #4: Do Not Defend Yourself

Then the fourth vow we must take is never to defend ourselves. I am not talking about the matter of war. I was in the Army during the First World War (not the Revolutionary War as you thought), and I had five sons in uniform in the Second World War, so I am not saying that it is not proper for us, when our country is threatened, to defend that country. We have all the benefits that this nation extends to us. Why then should we not help take care of it when it gets in danger?

But this is something else again. What I am talking about is that we, as individuals, are not to defend *ourselves*, but live in the Sermon on the Mount (Matthew 5:1-7:29). You know, they have taken the Sermon on the Mount and given it to the millennium; I am willing that the millennium should have the Sermon on the Mount, but I want a bit of it now. I believe it is for us now, not only, as one man says, a beautiful moral application. I believe that it is binding upon the children of God, and one thing it teaches is that we're not to fight back.

And so I say take this vow: do not defend yourself. I got into a jam one time that was not my fault at all; that is, it came from another direction. I was just crushed by it, and I went to God. I was reading in Exodus, and the Lord spoke to me just as clearly as if He had never said it to anybody else.

Did you ever have that happen? You go to some text, and some dispensationalist tells you it is not yours. Something in your heart leaps up and grabs it. You feel a sucking sound and a pop as your feet come out of the mud, and it got you out. Then you read a book that says it was not for you. I do not care about that.

But anyhow, the twenty-third chapter of Exodus (verses 20-24) said to me,

> Behold, I send an Angel before thee, to keep thee in the way, and to bring thee into the place which I have prepared. Beware of him, and obey his voice, provoke him not; for he will not pardon your transgressions: for my name is in him. But if thou shalt indeed obey his voice, and do all that I speak; then I will be an enemy unto thine enemies, and an adversary unto thine adversaries. For mine Angel shall go before thee, and bring thee in unto the Amorites, and the Hittites, and the Perizzites, and the Canaanites, and the Hivites, and the Jebusites: and I will cut them off. Thou shalt not bow down to their gods.

Do not run around apologizing and asking people, "Please forgive me for living, or I will drop dead tomorrow." Look at verse 24: "But thou shalt utterly overthrow them, and quite break down their images." Somebody called me an iconoclast, and I have biblical authority for it—the word means "destroyer of idols." God says here, "Utterly overthrow them and quite break down their idols."

I thought I was going to die at about thirty—I am fifty-five and still percolating—but He said, "I will take sickness away from the midst of thee. There shall nothing cast their young, nor be barren, in thy land: the number of thy days I will fulfil" (23:25-26). And that is as long as I want to live.

Verse 27 says, "I will send my fear before thee, and will destroy all the people to whom thou shalt come, and I will make all thine enemies turn their backs unto thee." God said that to me, and then He said this, and I am not sure but God may have a sense of humor too, because verse 28 cannot be explained unless there is just a wee little bit of humor in the heart of God. He said, "And I will send hornets before thee, which shall drive out the Hivite, the Canaanite, and the Hittite, from before thee."

Imagine the great God Almighty, who made the seven stars and rolled the Pleiades yonder, stooping to have a bee run interference for me. I stopped fighting right there. I stopped in principle. I admit I broke over sometimes, but every time I broke away I came back with a black eye, a bloody nose and a hurt heart.

I have a tongue like a rapier. God knows how long it has taken to sanctify it, and I am doubtful about it yet, but every time I have dared to use a hot tongue I have recoiled, and it took me days and months to get over it. God said He would do my fighting for me

(Exodus 14:14). If you insist on fighting, I warn you: you are up against a terrible enemy.

So if you hear something that is said about you, do not run around trying to straighten it out. It is just like trying to pick soot off the front of your white shirt—you just smear it around. Let it go; God will blow it off for you. It will not hurt you. Do not say, "It is not fair." The devil invented the phrase, "It is not fair." So take this vow before God never to defend yourself.

Vow #5: Never Take God's Glory

The fifth point is you must be sure never to take any of God's glory for yourself. When I was writing *Wingspread*,[4] an old man told me some things about Dr. A.B. Simpson. Some of the things he told me about Dr. Simpson I did not put in the book because they were not complimentary to the dear man—that he had a changeable mind; that he could not remember where his money had gone and all that sort of thing. He was not a wax saint at all. He was a man of like passions.

I said, "But brother, if Dr. Simpson was a man with such flaws in his makeup, why did God bless him so?"

The old man straightened up like a prophet and said, "Mr. Tozer, God knew that His glory was safe in the hands of A.B. Simpson. He knew that He could trust A.B. Simpson never to filch any of the honor that belonged to God."

The result was that with all of his flaws, God not only blessed Simpson but blasted any man that opposed him. Those are solemn, wonderful words. It is not flawlessness God is looking for; it is consecration to a point where we will never allow ourselves to steal a percentage of the honor that belongs to the most holy God. "Not unto us, Oh LORD, but unto Thy name give glory" (Psalm 115:1).

These five points are easy to remember. I promise you they are biblical, and if you put them in practice, taking them one at a time and praying them through until they become part of your nerves and blood—oh, what God may do with you dear people in the next few weeks, months and years!

But remember, you will violate them at your peril. You will shrink and shrivel and be small, and your fruit will be wormy, and your usefulness will be handicapped if you violate or ignore these things I have given you.

[This message was delivered at Wheaton College's Pierce Chapel on October 1, 1952.]

How to Be Filled with the Holy Spirit

C onservative, fundamental Christians all over
the world agree that we ought to be Spirit-
filled Christians. But there is very little counsel
given, so far as I can learn, on what it means and
how we can be filled with the Spirit and walk in
the Spirit. Today I want to bring serious counsel
on this topic, "How I might be filled with the
Spirit." What I have to say is not a sermon; rather,
it is serious spiritual counsel to Christians.

In Isaiah 8:13-14 are these words of God to the
man of God, "Sanctify the LORD of hosts himself; and
let him be your fear, and let him be your dread. And
he shall be for [you] a sanctuary." We can see from
the earlier part of the chapter that an invasion was
threatening. Assyria was to come in like a mighty
flood because the people had turned away from God.
Yet even with this invasion threatening, they were
still turning away from God and trying to meet the
invasion through an alliance of several nations. Only
Isaiah heard a voice—only Isaiah.

Every age has a few that hear the voice—God's
voice, and that alone. And only Isaiah saw the vision

of what could be. To this greatest of all prophets God spoke strongly (see Isaiah 8:11) and said, "Walk not in the ways of this people Israel." He was commanded to stand against the popular trend.

I do not like to say this, and I would not for the world say anything inadvertently that would make a rebel out of me. We have too many rebels, but they are mostly all rebels out of their own carnal heart. Nevertheless, there is such a thing as being a Protestant in the right sense of the word. There is such a thing as a quiet but firm and unshakable protest against the popular trend, even in religion.

The man of God was told that he could not afford to go along with the masses of Israel, to follow the popular trend, but that he was to "sanctify the LORD of hosts Himself," and God would be to him a sanctuary. This reveals that if we make God our fear and our dread, then we have a secret sanctuary in the midst of a violent and dangerous world; the result is a witness to all the world. It says further on in the chapter, "I will wait upon the LORD. . . and I will look for him. Behold, I and the children whom the LORD hath given me are for signs and for wonders in Israel from the LORD of hosts" (8:17-18). Isaiah's name lives on, and the names of these alliance chieftains, whoever they were, have all been forgotten.

Isaiah opens for us here the secret way to power. It is secret not in the esoteric sense, but it is secret because so few people know anything about it or desire to follow. It is to sanctify the Lord Himself; that is, to set God aside as being all in all, to throw ourselves over on God Himself, to recognize God as our all-ness, and in personal experience make God everything.

I suspect that this may sound rather dry to some of you young people whose blood runs hot and whose ambitions are high, but I must continue to say (for it is the Word of the Lord and is confirmed in tens of thousands of human hearts through the years) that anything you seek outside of God is wrong. No matter how shining it may seem to be, nor how utterly desirable, if it is outside of God, it is wrong. Anything that comes to your attention that is outside of God is wrong—only God is right, and only the will of God is safe, for the will of God is the help of the universe, and this moral sickness, this languishing sickness that is on the race is the result of the race getting out of the will of God. We are ill because we have violated the law of life which is the will of God.

Experiencing God

We can make God our personal experience. Again I will repeat, as I often do, that we are not to apologize for the word *experience*. I grew up, I regret, in an atmosphere where I was taught to be ashamed to use the word *experience*, because some old lady once climbed a tent pole or some fellows rolled in the straw at a camp meeting in some fanatical bush-whacking service somewhere. "That is *experience*," I was told. "You must preach the Bible, not experience."

I preach the Bible in order that we might have experience. Certainly experience that does not bring out the Bible is invalid and will disappoint us, but the Bible without experience confirmed to us individually is just so much theology, so much learned lumber crammed into our heads out of which we can make no sanctuaries.

I stress personal experience. There is such a thing as knowing God personally, having the experience yourself, having an encounter with God that is as bright and shining as any other experience in life—and much more so, because it engages a much more important Person. God will respond if we set Him aside in our heart. God, the all-embracing One, who fills all the world, is easily accessible. He is accessible to us in Christ.

I got my fingers burned by some modernist on that "in Christ" business, so I have another preposition. I say that God is not only accessible to us *in* Christ but He is accessible to us *as* Christ. I know it is possible to say I have found God in Christ, but I have read poems where a dear lady said she found God in a butterfly's wing or in a daisy, and I do not mean that when I say that we find God in Christ. I mean that we find God *as* Christ the Beloved. He is God acting the way God would act and doing what God would do and feeling as God feels and being what God is. So in Jesus Christ I find God, and He gives Himself to our faith as bread.

For years I experienced disappointment in the communion service. I could not understand and embrace transubstantiation or con-substantiation or any substantiation I had heard about. I just could not get hold of them somehow. Even our plain little unbeautiful communion services bothered me as lacking luster and failing to feed my heart.

Then one day in secret prayer God said to my heart, "Son, faith is eating, and when you gaze at Jesus Christ in faith you are partaking of Jesus Christ." After that I never had any more trouble at all because communion to me is partaking of Jesus Christ, the Bread of Life, with the mouth of faith—gazing upon Him and eating of Him, and having Him, and taking Him into my spiritual system by faith.

Faith is not something to be apologized for—it is a faculty of the human spirit. Just as the mouth takes food into the stomach, so faith, and the gaze of faith, takes in the Lord Jesus Christ. God Almighty is all to you and me. So I say that we can have Him through faith and love, and we actually do have God—not a shadow of God, not a picture of God, not an echo of God but God Himself as Christ.

Fearing God

The Scripture says, "Make God your fear, and make God your dread, and He will be to you a sanctuary" (Isaiah 8:13-14, author's paraphrase). In God is complete safety. Whoever fears God enough never needs to fear anyone or anything else.

One of the hardest words in the New Testament is in First John. It says, "Perfect love casteth out fear" (4:18). I have been afraid of everything that moved (and a lot of things that did not move) ever

since I can remember. I have never been coura-
geous, and I wondered how can it be possible that
perfect love will cast out fear? How can I ever get
enough love to cast out fear?

But I think I know now. It means if I fear God
enough—if I have that delighted, reverent, trem-
bling, holy dread in the presence of the holy
God—then I can, like Elijah, say, "I stand before
Jehovah" (1 Kings 17:1; 18:15; 2 Kings 3:14; 5:16).

Elijah was not afraid of King Ahab. Elijah was
not dressed for a court. He had never read an eti-
quette book, and he had never been briefed on
how to act in the presence of a king. He was a
great big awkward fellow who walked flat-footed
and, I suppose, had all the characteristics of the
mountains where he had been bred, but he had
absolutely no fear in the presence of Ahab. He
said, "I stand before Jehovah." That explains
why he was not afraid of a mere king. Elijah had
stood a lifetime in the presence of the mighty
King. If I fear God enough I never need to fear
anything else.

I need fear no one and no thing because no one
and no thing can finally injure me. I believe this
with all that is inside of me—nobody can harm
me. Put me in jail, yes, but not harm me; cut off
my head, yes, but not harm me; rob me but not
harm me; calumniate my name but not harm me;
for harm must be understood in the divine context. And only that which finally harms me harms
me at all. They can take my body and property
and all the rest, but if I wear the red mantle of His

holy shielding blood, I am a man as safe as if I had been in heaven for millenniums.

I want to say a word to young Christians, especially those who shall be missionaries and preachers. I urge you, take yourself out of the hands of men. God does not want us to be followers of men. He wants us to love them and to appreciate them and to admire them. He calls us to listen to them and to obey them if they have authority over us. God calls us to work with them and be harmonious and not be a rebel or assert our carnal individuality—He wants us to do all that. But He wants us to have a secret understanding with God so that we are in His hands.

I think one of the most pitiful things in the wide world is a little, jittery, frightened preacher just out of seminary trying to get himself a job—the best one available—and for that reason taking the district superintendent or bishop out to lunch. I think it is pathetic—absolutely pathetic. I find it hard to keep contempt out of my heart and voice when I talk about a man like that.

You do not have to do it, young person, you do not have to do it. As soon as you get proper training and get what you ought to know and get disciplined and taught how to think and learn the Word, then you look to heaven and say, "Now, God, I am ready." And then take the first thing God throws in your direction and go on from there. You never need to run around and polish the apple for the person that is next over you.

I also urge you to ignore their threats and their flattery. Those are the two sources of danger—flattery and abuse. I had a tough time getting over flattery, and I am not yet quite over it, but I am getting there. My hide is getting thicker year by year because I have discovered that only those who do not amount to much criticize me. By that neat little trick of psychology I manage to get along with everybody. I might be amazed to know how many good people criticize me, but they never tell me. But we must take ourselves out of the hands of men.

You say, "That is all right for an old fellow, but for me it is different—I am a young man."

No, it is not different for you. This is not for any age group. I think we make a mistake in dividing up spiritual experiences for different ages. Anything God can do for an older person He can do for a younger person, if the young person will concentrate and get sharply focused on God. That is the trouble with youth—they lack focus. Assemble yourselves sometime before God; get together once and look into the face of God. God will do anything for you that He did for anyone, regardless of age.

Refuse to leave yourself and your future in the hands of men. Seek advice, take counsel, work with people, but have a secret understanding with God: "Oh, Lord God, Thou art my all. Thou art my tomorrow as Thou art my yesterday and today. Thou art my here and my there, my now and my then. Thou art all in all to me; time and space converge upon Thee. All that I have or ever hope to be is Thine." You know, that works within a life; it gets within a life and works like a holy yeast within your spirit.

Everything in Christ

Let us think about God in Christ for a few moments. "Sanctify the LORD Himself." Sanctify Christ. Christ is the man-ward side of God. Christ is the side of God that looks toward the human race, and Jesus Christ is the way to God because He is Himself God. He is to our souls what our souls are to our bodies.

Far too often in our age, Jesus is confined to religion. Sometimes I feel like saying, "They have taken away my Lord, and I know not where they have laid him" (John 20:13). You go to conferences and hear about prophecy, baptism, Jewish history, doctrines; you might even get a little Greek and Hebrew thrown in for dessert. You will hear all about the shelves and scaffoldings of religion, and they are good and necessary—you cannot have a sanctuary without walls, and you cannot have the walls without the scaffolding while they are being built, but I do not want to live on a scaffolding all my life. I want to get in where the sanctuary is and kneel and adore.

Christianity, my friend, is dedicated to the adoration of Jesus Christ. It is not only to save you from the consequences of your sin, but to give you that which you were created to enjoy. It is to give you God. It is to break God down for you, so to speak, so that your created heart can get hold of God, so that the love of Jesus Christ will be real to you.

If you glance back over Church history you will find that almost all the mighty men whose names have come down to us—whose names we give to our babies, chapels and schools—were persons who had fallen delightfully in love with the person of Jesus Christ the Lord. They did not all agree on every point of doctrine. Jonathan Edwards and John Wesley would not have been caught dead in the same building if they had lived at the same time because one was a strong Calvinist and one was a happy Arminian. But they loved the same Savior, and so their hearts glowed and they blessed their generation and left behind them a stream of spiritual molten gold into which we dip down to this very day.

God never asked them what school of theology they belonged to, He asked them, "What think ye of my Son?" And they said, "Oh, God, we are in love with Him!" And God said, "All right then, I am too, and so we are agreed." God blessed them in spite of their little aberrations, even as He will bless us despite our shortcomings.

The love of Christ, I say, is the core of everything in the Christian faith. He is the complete solution—there is not a problem in your life but what He can solve it. If we throw ourselves out upon the Lord Jesus Christ, He is enough.

Christ Is Our Wisdom

Christ is made unto us wisdom for our pitiful ignorance. You know, friends, we just do not know how ignorant we are—we really do not. Somebody said that education is pushing back the frontiers of our ignorance—that is, the more we know, the more we know that we do not know. Einstein (or whoever your hero is in the intellectual world) only knows more than most of us just how little we do know.

When I go into a library, I always come out blue. It takes me an hour and a half to get back up and get happy again. I see the books I have not read, the things I do not know, the subjects I am completely ignorant of, and it bothers me. It humbles me, and that is good for me.

But nobody knows very much. Wisdom can only do a few things. If it were what it should be, it could teach us how to live forever, how to be free from pain, how to keep our loved ones always by our side and never lose them in death. But it cannot do any of those things. So it just excites us and keeps us occupied and away we go. But when it is all over we have not known what we really ought to know.

Jesus Christ is God's wisdom given to His people. Jesus Christ will not teach you mathematics or biology; you will have to learn that the hard way. But all the essential spiritual and moral wisdom that makes saints you will find in Jesus Christ, your Lord. You will find how to overcome the grave and how to overcome mortality. In Him you will gain immortality and all the dreams that every race has sought. All this you will find in the person of Jesus Christ, God's Son.

Christ Is Our Righteousness

Jesus Christ is made unto us righteousness for our innate wrongheadedness. I suppose even more than our pitiful ignorance is our inexcusable wrongheadedness and our evil because we are evil inherently and continually. "Jesus Christ," says Paul, "is made unto us . . . sanctification" (1 Corinthians 1:30) for our innate evil. He is made to us courage for our paralyzing fear, strength for our utter weakness, life for our helpless dying.

Jesus Christ is life—even a better life than we lost. He is that eternal life. We may say, "God gives me eternal life, so now I have it." But eternal life is not life that lasts always—it does that too—but it is the *life* of the *eternal*. "And this is life eternal, that they might know [have correspondence with] thee, the only true God, and Jesus Christ, whom thou hast sent" (John 17:3).

Eternal life is an everlasting right adjustment to God through Jesus Christ, just as eternal death is to be cut off from God. When God gives me eternal life, He does not give me a *thing* at all—He gives me a Person. Jesus is that life, and He is our eternal life, wisdom, righteousness, sanctification, courage, strength—our all in all.

So I urge you to fall in love with the Son of God. You will find in Jesus Christ power; you will find in Him everything that those who do not understand this are seeking out of Him. The fellow who has a particular hobby—what he is seeking out there on the fringes, you have got right in the center. That which he is trying to do way out there in the woods, you have here in the sanctuary.

David said, "Then I understood when I went into the sanctuary" (Psalm 73:17, author's paraphrase). You will have more understanding in the sanctuary than anyplace else. There, in what the old writers call the *penetralia*, the deep inner part of your spirit, Jesus Christ will reveal Himself in all that God is to your soul, and you will find a treasure in Jesus Christ. Sanctify Jesus Christ; set Him apart; attach yourself to Him; dedicate yourself to Him; cut all the lines that bind you away from Him. Make Him your all in all, and He will become to you all that your happiest dream could conceive of Him, for Jesus Christ is wisdom and righteousness and sanctification and redemption.

> O Jesus, Jesus, dearest Lord!
> Forgive me if I say,
> For very love, Thy sacred name
> A thousand times a day.[1]

Jesus Christ is all and everything. Have you found Him? Is He yours? He is not a church (and I believe in churches); not a religion (and I believe in the Christian religion); He is Jesus Himself, the Bread of Life, the Sun, the Star, your All-in-All. Will you now dedicate yourself to Him?

[This sermon was given at Wheaton College, Pierce Chapel, on October 2, 1952.]

Be Filled with the Spirit

I think I have never said anything to you as important as what I am planning on saying tonight. I want to use this simple and very familiar text: "Be not drunk with wine, wherein is excess; but be filled with the Spirit" (Ephesians 5:18).

What I will say (outside of some notions I might import, which can scarcely be avoided as long as we are on earth and human) is nothing new, nothing strange, nothing extreme, nothing fanatical, nothing that you cannot believe and experience and stay in any gospel church in the world. It is nothing that is not believed by every fundamentalist or conservative Bible Christian in the world.

The difference is that I insist, if it is true, we ought to do something about it. That is all. I just bring in from the perimeter, the outer edge of things, a truth that is believed by everybody and hold it on me like a white light and insist, "Let us make this work; let us do something about this!"

"Be filled with the Spirit." You can call it "be getting filled" or "be being filled," and it adds up to the same thing. It is the will of God that His people should be Spirit-filled people—all of them, not only missionaries and preachers, but all of God's people everywhere.

I also have four other texts, and I am going to give them at the close of this message. This will be the first time you ever heard anybody preaching a sermon where there were four points in the conclusion and only one in the body of the sermon. It may confuse the homiletical department, but at least I will be getting across what I want to say.

I do not think that we are quite ready. I do not find Christians ready as a rule—the rank and file, average, good Christians—to hear the simple biblical way of being filled with the Spirit, because there are a number of things we need to get settled. First, we need to be sure that we can be filled with the Spirit. This would seem to be unnecessary since Paul commands us to be filled; and yet this whole topic has been so confused by the devil and by weird and strange men who let their flesh go that good, honest Christians have been frightened and driven away from the green pastures. The devil has frightened them and told them there were serpents hidden in the grass.

You can be, as a Christian, filled with the Holy Spirit. Every Christian has the Spirit or he could not be a Christian. We are baptized into the body of Christ by the Holy Spirit and made members of the body by the work of the Spirit uniting us to the body of Christ in regeneration. "If any man have not the Spirit of Christ, he is none of his" (Romans 8:9), and Christ dwells in us unless we are reprobates (2 Corinthians 13:5). I think that ought to settle that. Every Christian does have a measure of the Spirit.

But you must be convinced that it is God's will for you to be filled with the Spirit—that it is a part of the total plan of redemption, that when He said, "It is finished," He included this. You have got to be convinced of this or you will have no faith concerning it. You must believe that this is not abnormal or unusual; in fact, it is abnormal *not* to be Spirit-filled. God means His people to be Spirit-filled, and the abnormalities within the Church are where we are not Spirit-filled.

We must also be sure, restfully sure, that there is nothing strange or weird about all this, but that it is God Almighty's plan for all of His children to be filled with the Spirit and walk in the Spirit. We have got to be sure to the point of conviction, because if we are not sure we cannot possibly exercise faith.

We must be sure that there is no need to persuade God. We need not come to God and ask Him to do something that He has declared He is willing to do, or try to coax God into a frame of mind that He has been in since the beginning of the world. Unless we are restfully convinced of this, I recommend that you do not do anything at all except search the Scriptures, meditate on the Scriptures bearing this truth, remain calm and confident, and put away fear and worry and irritation, because these are never of God.

The Holy Spirit is the Comforter; He comforts the heart. Where there is panic and intimidation and great fear, we may be sure we are victims of an overheated imagination or of the devil himself, because the blessed Lord Jesus never irritated anybody except bad men. When willing, hungry people came, no matter how sinful, no matter how far from the truth, no matter how far down in the moral gutter, the Lord Jesus Christ tenderly helped them and never turned an angry face to a seeking heart. He sent Pharisees, scribes, Saducees and liars away licking their wounds every time. But if your heart is tender toward God and you only want the will of God, you will get the kind, courteous treatment that our Lord Jesus Christ is famous for. Always you will get it from Him.

You must not only know and be sure that you can be filled with the Spirit as a Christian, but you must desire to be. Here I will run into the first real question you will have in your mind: "Mr. Tozer, would you waste our time and yours by saying that we must be sure that we desire to be? Why, *everybody* desires to be filled with the Spirit!"

I am not sure of that at all. If they do, it is not a conclusive or inclusive desire; it is a fugitive longing rather than a desire. Everybody is as holy as he wants to be, and everybody is as full as he wants to be. It has to be so, because our Lord said, "Blessed are they which do hunger and thirst after righteousness: for they shall be filled" (Matthew 5:6), and the filling is in exact proportion to the hunger. So if we are not filled, it is because we are not sufficiently hungry.

One of the old saints of God, in generations gone by, had the reputation for being a very godly man and for being able to help people with the Word. Young folks and students and young preachers from afar would come to him and he would just give them a word and send them away. It was a gift of God to the man.

One day two young preachers came to see him who had walked a long way. He walked out to meet them, greeted them and said, "You are as holy as you want to be; good-bye." He turned away and closed the door.

They looked at each other, walked slowly down the steps and told it all around everywhere. "This man, we went to him for help, and he just said, 'You are as holy as you want to be,' and brought the interview to a conclusion." Well, it worked, all right, and it is true. Everybody *is* as holy as he wants to be. When I say "want to be" I mean "*really* want to be"—to a point where it burns in your heart.

The old devotional writers used to say that desiring and receiving are all one piece. In God they were not separated. One end of a pencil is the desire, the other end of the pencil is the receiving of the desire, and they are always together. You cannot separate them because since Christ died on the cross and the holy Comforter has come, all grace is to us-ward and all has been taken out of the way by the blood of the Lamb. There is nothing standing in the way but our lack of desire.

Consequently, the desiring and the receiving are all one piece. It is said, "You have some feeling of God or you would not want any more of God. The fact that you desire God proves that you have some of God." That is good, biblical teaching, brethren, and so I say you must desire to be filled.

Let us examine the extent of your desire. Do you want to be possessed by a spirit who is like Jesus—pure, gentle, sane, wise, healing and loving—but who will nevertheless be Lord of your life? Jesus exercises His lordship through the Holy Ghost; He cannot exercise it any other way. Therefore, the Spirit of God will demand to be Lord of your life. Do you truly want to be in gentle and loving possession of an indwelling Spirit that will be Lord over you (that will make Jesus be Lord over you, to be technically correct)?

It seems to me that it is here where some of us stick. We want to be saved, but we want to be lord over our lives. That is at the threshold of life; we must be willing that the Holy Spirit become, in Jesus' stead, Lord over our lives.

Next, are you sure you want a personality to take possession of your personality? Let me describe Him and what He will do: He will expect obedience to the written Word and to the living Word in heaven. He will expect obedience from you, and He will not tolerate in you the self-sins. He will not tolerate self-love. He will not tolerate self-righteousness. He will not tolerate self-indulgence, not any of the hyphenated sins that have self in them. He will deal with them, and He will bring you to repentance. He will chastise and discipline until He gets your consent to take them out of your life. He will not live with them. He will not move in where these self-sins are in fullness of measure. Although, as I say, He certainly dwells somewhere in the recesses of every believer's heart or that person would not be a believer indeed.

You will find this blessed Holy Spirit in sharp opposition to the world's easy ways. We live in a degenerate hour when Christianity, it seems to me, needs a mighty reviving from somewhere, for the business of the Church now seems to be to get along with the world and to go the world's way with the least possible opposition.

But the Holy Ghost says, "Never mind the opposition of the world." He expects it, just as Jesus Christ in whom He dwells in fullness of perfection experienced opposition as long as He lived on earth, and just as the Church that names His name has had it wherever she has been a pure and holy Church. Instead of your taking Christianity and molding it to fit the world to avoid the disgrace of the cross, the Holy Ghost will insist that you leave it as it is and walk with God in the light of New Testament truth without caring what the world says about you.

Such a lifestyle will bring you into conflict with the world, for the ways of God and the ways of man do not parallel each other. They intersect each other, and where their intersection is there will be heat, friction, opposition, trouble and maybe persecution.

The Holy Spirit will not allow you to boast or show off or strut or shine. Much of modern Christianity is run by strutters and shiners and show-offers, but "we are persuaded better things

of you, and things that accompany salvation"
(Hebrews 6:9). I do not believe that you want it
that way. God will not allow you to boast. If you
do catch yourself boasting, you will feel tough
inside until you have lifted your heart and said,
"Forgive me, God." He will not allow you to seek
a place in the sun or show off or seem to be
somebody. He will put humility in you and insist on keeping it there.

The Holy Spirit will also take the direction of
your life away from you. I have practically said
that before when I said that He would be Lord of
your life. He will reserve the right to discipline
you and strip you, maybe, of some things you
think are indispensable. He might even hurt you a
little in the process, as a father must a child for the
child's everlasting good. I do not leave the impres-
sion that you will always be standing in the corner
under the discipline of God, but I do mean to say
that when it is necessary you will.

When the Spirit deals with you, you will be a disciple, and He may strip away from you many loved
and dangerous things—things that you think are
harmless but that He knows are deadly. He will take
them away from you as He took Isaac away from
Abraham, and yet purified their relationship and
gave Isaac back; that is always God's way.

The thing that you hold in your own right may
be dangerous, but once God has broken your heart
and taken it away from you He may give it back to
you, and it's perfectly harmless after God pulls its
sting. Ultimately, He does not care what you have,

but He has to pull its sting first. He has to pull the poison fangs out of it, and then He hands it back and says, "Now use this for My glory." Whatever it may be—a gift, a girlfriend, an ambition, a desire for some kind of work, a possession—whatever it may be, as long as you hold it, it has got a poison tail on it, but God will take it, purify it, hand it back and say, "There, now you can have it, because I have disciplined out of you the thing that made it dangerous in you."

Not only must you be sure that you can be filled with the Spirit and sure that you desire to be, but you must be sure that you *need* to be. Can you not get along all right by yourself? Most Christians can; that is why we are in the fix we are in now. That is why the world is laughing at us; that is why we are imitators and not initiators. That is why we keep an eye on the latest from Hollywood and Broadway and then create something religious—a weak imitation of Frank Sinatra or somebody else.

There was a day when the world followed the Church. She took the initiative; she was aggressive. But it has changed now, and we are down on our knees imitating the world. The Church is like a poor old withered hag, rather than the beautiful, full-blooded bride of the Lamb we are intended to be. That we should stand by the world's highway and stretch out our withered hand for a dime from the world is a disgrace.

There was a day when the Church could say, "Silver and gold have I none; but such as I have give I thee . . . rise up and walk" (Acts 3:6). Today the Church says, "Now, now, please do not take me wrong: I think the same as you only I have Jesus; that is the difference. I am just like you only I have Jesus." That is the kind of unholy, unscriptural, hybrid mongrel Christianity that we are propagating at great expense and time and labor in our day. The Christianity of the cross never tries to please the world, but dares to stand on its two legs and let the world come around.

Emerson, down on a lower level, said, "Plant yourself on your instincts and the world will come around to you." The Church of Jesus in the early days never tried to please the world. The Church planted itself on its spiritual instincts, took God and the cross and said, "Here we are; we can be nothing else, so help us God," and the world came around to them.

Can you get along on the dead level? If you can, then I have nothing much to say to you, only God bless you; sleep well. But I wonder if you can really get along well the way you are. If you can, then all right, pay no attention. If we cannot agree, then we will not disagree. We will still nod and smile as we pass each other.

But do you feel you can go on the way you are and resist discouragement, obey the word, understand the truth, bring forth fruit, live in victory, win men to God, die in peace and meet Christ with joy? Do you think you can do that in the state you are in now? I do not think you can, and I do not think you think you can. I think we all have to say, "If thy presence go not with [us], carry us not up hence" (Exodus 33:15). If God does not fill us, then please God, do not expect anything of us, for You know us. You know that in our hearts "dwelleth no good thing" (Romans 7:18).

This desire, and I am assuming now you have it, must become all-absorbing. It must be for the time the biggest thing in your life. If there is anything bigger, then you will have very little satisfaction in the realm of which I speak. I am not sure that anybody has ever been Spirit-filled who did not first go through a time of disturbance and anxiety. That does not contradict what I said before, for it is a holy, healing anxiety; at the same time there is a sense of God's being there. It is not despair, but it is disturbance and disappointing emptiness.

Perhaps you remember a classic illustration of Moody, the self-assured man, who was out preaching and winning souls. Then Mother Cook told him, "Son, what you need is to be filled with the Spirit." He had not yet had the idea that he could be filled educated out, fought out or beaten out of him, so he believed her.

"I never changed a sermon," he later said, "but a wonderful new power came into the ones that I had been preaching."

That, I say, is a classic example of a spiritual experience. But there came that disappointing emptiness when he knew that the man who was beginning to get the attention of the Christian world was not what he should be. Disappointing emptiness, I say. Some people want to be blessed all the time. If they cannot be blessed all the time, they are unhappy, bothering God about it, worrying and saying, "Now, God, I do not feel as good today as I did at 4 o'clock yesterday. What is the matter here?"

We spend our time chinning ourselves on religious bars, pulling ourselves up and letting ourselves down all the time. Do not be afraid of feeling bad; do not be afraid of letting God come into your soul and do some plowing. You cannot have fruit or grain until you do some plowing. God may even send somebody to do the plowing whom you do not like at all and think is unworthy to run a plow over you. David said, "The plowers plowed upon my back: they made long their furrows" (Psalm 129:3).

God did not do it; He just sent a fellow that David did not like to do it. You see, if God always came in royal dignity, waved His wand and allowed us to stand there like we were having our picture taken, that would be all right—but we would go to heaven proud as Lucifer. So the Lord may let somebody come along that is no good, some preacher (maybe like me) and just plow your back a little. You think, "Why, that fellow does not know as much as I know, and here you are sending him, God, to plow me." So humble yourself and let God plow you, and do not be afraid of emptiness.

The saints of God have all had to go through those times of emptying out, those times of getting rid of that Adamic bounce. You know, that Adamic bounce to the ounce that comes as standard equipment. We have got it; we cut its hair differently and give it another name, but it is old Adam nonetheless. It is old self-confidence. Especially if he has read a book, and he is so sure of himself, but he is old Adam, nevertheless, and God has been finished with Adam ever since the day that He cast him out of the garden.

God said to Noah, "The end of all flesh is come before me" (Genesis 6:13). He slays the flesh and raises the man up in newness of life. Dying is not easy. I have not died in the physical sense, but I have been through some dying in the interior sense, and I well know it is not easy.

That is why I never could follow this "happified" Christianity. There is "joy unspeakable and full of glory" (1 Peter 1:8); there is rapture and flights of spiritual delight; there is joy in the Holy Ghost; there is sweet, healing worship; there is all that in the Church of God. But it is on another level; it is a spiritual thing. It is something that has gone into the grave and come out again.

But the poor Church in our day does not know that, so she is importing her joy for ten cents a dozen from the world and then tagging the name "Jesus" onto it, saying, "Now we're religious." You are not religious—it is just old Adam with another tag on him. You can get that same kind of thrill in a nightclub—they play certain music and say, "That sends me." I have seen religious meetings that were just "sent," that was all.

But there is another kind of joy, the joy that seeks me through pain, "the joy that was set before him" that enabled Him to endure the cross (Hebrews 12:2). Once you have tasted of that joy, you'll smile at any other kind of joy. You may have to go through a time of skinning and of harming and injuring old Adam, but Jesus Christ your Lord will be with you. He went through that way first and came out, and now He is in glory forevermore, "bringing many sons unto glory" (2:10) and teaching them obedience by the things they suffer (5:8).

All this that I am talking about—the destruction of my natural and boisterous life, my human confidence and all the rest—does not earn any gift for me, and it does not make me dear to God. I have been dear to God since the beginning of the world and before, but it does break up the plot of ground, and it does empty the vessel.

D.L. Moody, when he preached on these things, used to take two glasses and a pitcher of water and he would try to pour water into a full glass. He would say, "You cannot get water into a glass that is full." Then he would pour it out and say, "Now it can be filled!" You can only fill an empty vessel. That rollicking camp meeting song we sing sometimes, "Bring your empty earthen vessels," is very true to the Scriptures. You have to be empty. If there is anything hidden there, God cannot fill you very full, so empty your hearts.

To return to the question, how can I be filled with the Spirit? I give you four texts. You can think them over and pray over them. First, Romans 12:1-2:

I beseech you therefore, brethren, by the mercies of God, that ye present your bodies a living sacrifice, holy, acceptable unto God, which is your reasonable service. And be not conformed to this world: but be ye transformed by the renewing of your mind, that ye may prove what is that good, and acceptable, and perfect, will of God.

"Present your bodies"—that is, present an empty vessel. Do not present a full vessel or an unclean vessel. Present a vessel where the blood of Jesus has cleansed away the stains, and you have said to Him, "Pardon, oh, Lord, my transgressions and have mercy upon me according to Thy righteousness and wash away all my sins." Present a clean vessel.

Second, Luke 11:9, 11-13:

Ask, and it shall be given you; seek, and ye shall find; knock, and it shall be opened unto you. . . . If a son shall ask bread of any of you that is a father, will he give him a stone? Or if he ask a fish, will he for a fish give him a serpent? If ye then, being evil, know how to give good gifts unto your children: how much more shall your heavenly Father give the Holy Spirit to them that ask him?

There are two ways to look at this text. The first is the way it is now being interpreted so as to destroy all its meaning; the second is in the light of Christian experience down through the centuries. Certain interpreters say this cannot possibly be a spiritual principle laid down, so they dismiss it. These interpreters, as a rule, seem to me to be more determined to prove a point than to be Christlike—more determined to interpret a verse in line with preconceived theology than to be filled with the Holy Ghost. The lips that usually speak against this are pretty cold lips.

But over against men's interpretations which say this is not for us is the long line of superior saints, prophets, reformers, missionaries, evangelists, pastors and holy people of God down through the years who have not been told that it is wrong to open your vessel and say, "Fill me, Lord." But I have been hearing that it is wrong to do it. I know better because I asked, and He gave me.

Third, Acts 5:32:

> . . . the Holy Ghost, whom God hath given to them that obey him.

He gives the Holy Spirit to them that obey Him. I have covered that, but it is the third point in my little talk.

Fourth, Galatians 3:2. Paul says,

> This only would I learn of you, Received ye the Spirit by the works of the law, or by the hearing of faith?

It is a rhetorical question. The answer is, "By the

hearing of faith, of course." Faith alone is the vessel that can receive. Faith alone can open the tap and fill with the Spirit. I want to watch my language, for I do not want to leave a sentence with you that Satan could twist or harm, so when I say receive I do not mean receive in the sense that He is far away and must come to your heart. I mean receive or be filled in the sense that He fills His people with the Holy Spirit. Even after Pentecost it was written that "Peter, filled with the Holy Ghost, said . . ." (Acts 4:8). There was nothing incompatible with sound theology embraced by the apostles, surely, and they were filled, sometimes, with the Holy Ghost.

God wants to fill you. I give you this, and here is the only place I expect to run into trouble with some of you good, careful Bible expositors, but I give you this and I do not give you the text, so if you want to disbelieve me, we will still be friends. I have not heard that anyone ever was filled who did not know he had been, and I have never heard of anybody being filled gradually.

You think with me for a moment about the Old Testament and the New Testament—do you ever remember of any place in the Old Testament when the Holy Spirit came gradually? No place. Ever hear of any place in the New Testament where He came gradually? No, He did not. I do not say that God never did. But I do say He never recorded an instance where He did. Always the Holy Spirit is self-announcing and self-validating; you do not have to be told.

A great man of God who is now in heaven and

whom Dr. Edman[1] and I greatly admire once preached from the text, "Out of his belly shall flow rivers of living water" (John 7:38). And some dear brethren, careful expositors, took him to lunch afterwards. After they had gotten him nicely settled, the soup had been disposed of and they were ready for the main course, they said, "Now, dear brother, we think that was a good sermon, but oh, you were woefully unbiblical in your exegesis. That did not mean what you thought it meant at all." (He had taught that they would be filled with the Spirit, and out from within them would flow rivers of living water.)

They said, "That does not mean that. We will show you what that means dispensationally." They went along and dispensationalized a while. Pretty soon one of them got honest with himself and came down off his theological pedestal. He bowed his head and the tears began to flow. He said, "Brother, we have the right exegesis, but you have the rivers." I would rather have the rivers than the right exegesis. But I am not apologizing for bad exegesis, either! I think I have given you a fair presentation.

If we do not believe this, let us stop singing "Fill Me Now" and all those revival hymns and choruses. Let us stop it and be honest with ourselves. If it is not biblical and the belief in it is unscriptural, let us take it out of our hymnbooks. Why sing in our hymnbooks what we deny in our lives?

But if it is true, then let us begin to expect wondrously that He will "Fill Me Now" with Himself.

Are you with me on this? Is not this more than anything else—that God should give you full increased measures of His blessed Holy Spirit to be your Comforter, your Mentor, your Inner Teacher, your Guide, to give you an unction from the Holy One? While your teacher is teaching your intellect, this Holy One is teaching your heart, to keep, rebuke, encourage and comfort you—that is what He is here for. Oh, we have neglected Him so shamefully. We have forgotten Him days without end. Let us not do it any more. Let us expect Him to fill us.

[This message was delivered at Pierce Chapel, Wheaton College, on the evening of October 2, 1952.]

How to Cultivate the Spirit's Companionship

I plan to follow last night's topic by speaking to-night on "How can I cultivate the Spirit's companionship?" The text is found in Amos, a little-known and appreciated book, the third chapter, the third verse. It says, "Can two walk together, except they be agreed?" This is a rhetorical question. The answer is implied, and the question is the answer. It is equivalent to a positive declaration that two cannot walk together except they be agreed.

For two people to walk together there must be agreement on at least a few major points. They must be agreed on the direction. If one man is going north and one is going south it is a physical impossibility that they could walk together. They must also be agreed on their destination. If they were aiming for two different cities, they would have to separate somewhere on their journey. They are going to have to agree on what path they want to take. There might be a dozen paths to where they are going, and if they are going to stay together they are going to have to take the same path.

They will have to agree on the rate of speed. If one of them is a Theodore Roosevelt and believes in the strenuous life, he will walk very rapidly. Another man might saunter along. While they would ultimately get to the same place, they could not go together because they would have to agree upon the rate of speed.

Then they will have to agree whether they *want* to walk together. I know lots of people who, if I were going somewhere, I would like to walk with. Then I know others that for certain reasons I could not be comfortable with, because when I would rather look at the trees they would want to talk and talk. In brief, people have to agree that there would be advantage in their walking together. There would have to be some kind of compatibility.

I cannot conceive of a man who was utterly absorbed in photography—who would pull out a light meter at the drop of a hat—walking very far with a baseball fan who knows all the batting averages of the sixteen clubs. They would make it a while, but pretty soon it would get tiresome. They would have to have some common ground upon which they could agree or their walk would be one long boredom. You see what I mean. For two to walk together voluntarily, they must in some sense be one. The point here bears on the message of "How to walk with God in the Spirit and have fellowship with Jesus Christ."

I might also say that some people are not ready for this. Our Lord said that there were certain things He could not tell them (John 16:12). Paul said, "I could not talk to you as unto grownups; I had to talk to you as unto children" and he further noted that, "You are even now children" to a certain church to which he wrote (see 1 Corinthians 3:1-2). Nevertheless, I have discovered that if I focus my talk on the immature Christians, those who are eager to grow fail to get any place.

We are just going to have to write off to breakage some people. We must simply say, "Well, the eggs were delivered; there were a certain number of them that were spoiled. Hatch the ones that will hatch." There are some of you, God bless you, who will never go out and settle down. Unfortunately, you will become just one more church member. I am sorry, but a crowd like this always has a bunch of fringe hanger-oners like that. I do not know who you are but I know you are here. Thank God there are not very many like that, I trust, in an audience such as Wheaton can assemble.

For those who are not ready, I would further say that they want Christianity for its insurance value. What they get out of it is insurance against hellfire and a home in heaven at last. They are willing to inconvenience themselves twice a Sunday for that kind of insurance. They will put some money into it and abstain from certain grosser pleasures. They will also endure certain minor inconveniences in order to keep up their insurance, so they will know that when they die at last they will go to heaven and make it in.

The conception of religion for some is social, not spiritual. They water down the Word of God and

the long line of New Testament truths with their
own easygoing opinions, mixing them up together.
These people are not ready to hear what I have to
say. Judging from the people who have spoken to
me, I think there is a vast number here ready to
hear what I have to say about how we can cultivate the Spirit's companionship.

The Holy Spirit is a living Person. We must get
that straight. He is a living Person. I bought a big,
monstrous book of religious poetry here this week
and had it over in my room. When I had nothing
better to do I took a look in it, and I will say there
is some religious poetry that I cannot figure at all.
The man or woman who wrote it must have been
busy at the time. The poem, having neither arms
nor legs, nor hands nor feet, is a vacuum. It is the
spirit of the universe or some such thing, and I
cannot figure it out.

But whenever God is known as a Person, I can
get my teeth in it because I know what they are
talking about. We must not allow our religious life
to peter out into poetic fancies. We must start by
bringing it to the Bible and believing biblical truth
and what it says about God. This Holy Spirit
which I preached last night and have mentioned
and emphasized a lot during my talks is a Person,
One with the Father and the Son.

Again I say that if we are going to walk with
Him in agreement, we are going to have to honor
and be engrossed with the Lord Jesus Christ. "For
the Holy Ghost was not yet given," it said, "because that Jesus was not yet glorified" (John 7:39).

It is the office and present work of the Holy Ghost to glorify and honor the Person of Jesus Christ our Lord. The Holy Spirit must speak about Himself or the Bible could not have been written. But He speaks not on His authority, but on the authority of the Savior from which He proceeds.

The more we know of the Holy Ghost the better we will know Jesus, and we cannot know Christ at all, really, except we know Him by the Holy Ghost. "No man can say that Jesus is the Lord, but by the Holy Ghost" (1 Corinthians 12:3). The Holy Spirit is here to show us the lovely face of Jesus. The more I glorify Jesus Christ, love Him, make much of Him, obey Him, pray to Him and read His Book, the more the Holy Spirit will manifest Him to me and the closer I will know this Holy One who is the Holy Ghost.

He will relax, lull and commune with us and then indeed we can say, "Oh, Invisible, we see Thee; Intangible, we feel Thee; Inaudible, we hear Thee." It will not be a polite fancy but a sharp reality. It will be as real to us as the trees out upon the campus and the hand we put before our face. If we talk to Him and cultivate His knowledge, we must make our thoughts a clean sanctuary.

There is an amplified psychology school of thought whose followers are always working on their brain cells and saying that every day in every way we are getting better and better. I reject all that. I will not monkey with my own head. I do not know what I would find, and I am not too much interested, but your total religious thoughts are to a large degree under your control. God has made your thoughts a part of you.

"Thoughts," said somebody, "are things." The Spirit of God is in the world, and He is all-seeing, all-hearing and all-loving, but He knows your thoughts. A thought that enters the mind furtively, a fugitive thought that flies in and out, does not matter. But the thought you agree with and nurture and allow to perch and live within your mind becomes a part of you after a while.

God reckons you for what your thoughts are. Your thoughts must be a sanctuary, a holy place, for God cannot dwell in blood cells and nerve ends. He dwells in our thoughts, our will, our affections and our intellect. He dwells in the personality of us, rather than in the flesh and blood of us. When He says He will come in and dwell with us, certainly He dwells in our bodies, because our personalities are in our bodies, but He dwells deeper than in our bodies. He dwells in our personalities.

Therefore, if we are going to walk with Him and agree with Him, we are going to have to keep our personalities clean. He will not put up with malice, egotism, deceit, folly and sly, filthy talk. He will go silent on you and withdraw His sweet, sensitive presence. He will leave you on your own— He will be there but He will be there injured.

If you are going to walk with Him, then you must agree with Him. He is a *Holy* Spirit and you must keep your mind clean and your thoughts clean. Whatever you muse upon has got to be pure and hallowed, for He wants a hallowed sanctuary.

He will make the place of His feet glorious, and wherever His feet dwell, there is shining light and beauty and glory. Jesus Christ is that kind of Being; He will flee from the other kind of being. The profaned and polluted temple the Spirit will not dwell in.

What about borderline worldliness and its effect? I cannot lay down a rule for you that you can do this and cannot do that. But I can say this: quit whatever hinders your spiritual progress. This is a good, general working rule for your spiritual life, and this is the general essence of what God's Book says on this subject. Does this injure my heart? If it does, then it is not for me.

You say, "I know somebody who practices that and thinks nothing of it." You are not responsible for your brother's conscience. You are only responsible for your own. If this slows down *my* progress, then it is not for me, and I must get rid of it.

For instance, a great many years ago, when I was first getting acquainted with the great literature of the world, I ran across *Pepys' Diary*.[1] I thought that because it came in an artificial leather binding and was called a classic I ought to get acquainted with the great literature of the world. I read *Pepys' Diary*, but it bothered me. I liked it, but I did not like it. I would say to myself, "Now listen, you ought not to be a prude, nor a fanatic; you are going to have to get acquainted with what the great minds of the world have said." Pepys' mind was supposed to have been great, even though dirty, and so I went on reading *Pepys' Diary*. Every time I

came away from a session of *Pepys' Diary* I would
be less a Christian than I was before, so one day,
like Luther when he threw the inkwell at the devil,
I grabbed *Pepys' Diary*, ripped it to pieces and
hurled it in the wastebasket. I have never owned a
copy since.

I do not say *you* have to go to that extreme, but I
say that is what *I* had to do. I found lots of other
books beside *Pepys' Diary* that were not dirty. People want to know if they ought to read John Steinbeck.[2] If you like to wade knee-deep in obscenity,
read John Steinbeck. But if you do not, then let
Johnny alone, because he dipped his pen in the
distilled essence of obscenity and wrote his books,
and they have taken him on and made him a big
shot in his own right. He is a filthy man, and I
would not for the wide world be caught feeling my
way through the obscene recesses of his brain, because I will not read him. I read one and that was
enough.

I have to read those things that minister to my
own spiritual good. I will not filthy up my mind
with things that are not good for me. Maybe I am
off the track here, but I am here to talk to you
about the things that are on my heart, and this is
one of them. If it is hurting your spiritual life, drop
it. There is no rule. Maybe John Steinbeck would
not hurt you but he does not do me any good.
Maybe old Pepys would not hurt you a peep, but
he hurt me, and I dropped him.

I got dizzy here some years ago. When I would
get up quick, my head would go around and I

would see spots and not know what had happened to me. So I went to a doctor. He happened to be a crusty old fellow and he knew my dyspeptic kind as soon as he saw me.

I said, "My head whirls and I am dizzy. I do not understand it; I have never had anything like this before."

"Have you been eating anything unusual lately?"

"Well, to tell the truth I have," I said. "A few days ago I got a run on bananas, and I have been eating bananas at every meal."

And he said, "You've got blind staggers from eating bananas. Quit your bananas."

I quit my bananas and in a few days my blind staggers were gone too. I do not say you cannot eat bananas. I happen to know that I cannot. I can eat one, maybe, in a month, but I cannot eat them three times a day, because if I do I will get blind staggers. Up to that time I thought only mules got blind staggers, but I found preachers can get blind staggers too, on bananas, so I quit. That is just common sense. If they give me a dizzy head, quit them.

It is the same with other things. If you find they are hurting your spiritual life, it is your business to drop them now. Others may do what you cannot. If you are going to walk with God in the sweet fellowship of the Spirit, then you are going to have to be obedient and drop the things that displease God.

"But Mr. Tozer," you may say, "you mean to tell me I am going to have to give up things? Do you not think it is a bit unfair to demand of me that I give up things? And if I do not do the things others do I will be considered queer and laughed at."

Isn't that too bad—they will laugh at you! Well, you can always cry in your handkerchief, you know—and I recommend a pink one with perfume on it!

Dear God, what a bunch of sissies we are in this day! They crucified Jesus, ran a sword through James, cut off Paul's head and killed every one of the apostles except John, whom they exiled. The hot tongue, the cold shoulder and the sword have followed the cross of Jesus down through the years. We can go knock our teeth out in a football game and go to war and fight in blood and mire, and then when somebody says, "Well, you have got to be different and stand for the cross of Jesus," we whimper on our shoulder and say, "Can you not make it easier for us? It is just unfair that anybody should laugh at me." Oh, how little do I care if they laugh at me!

Paul Rader[3] used to tell about the boy who stood on the sidewalk with his face against a fence and every once in a while would jump and scream and yell. Then he would get his place again, looking through the fence. Somebody came by and saw him. He could not see anything except the boy going off into explosions of excitement, and he thought, "What in the world is the matter with that boy? Is he a little off?" Then he found the boy was looking through a hole in the fence and watching a baseball game. Every time the home team would come to bat and whack a homer, he would let go. He was seeing what was invisible to the other man, and he did not care what anyone else thought of him.

The man who walks with God truly walks with the invisible, and the world says he is crazy. But you see, a crazy person is one who reacts without any stimulus. Excuse my psychology, but he gets miserable or happy over something that does not exist. But a sane man is one whose reactions correspond to what is there. The Christian sees what is there, and his heart goes out to it. While the world does not see it and laughs at him, he sees it and knows what he sees. What do we care what they say about us? I hope I may never be caught whimpering, because it is certainly not worthy of the Christian.

I will go on to say that if we are to walk with Him, we must seek Him in the Word, for He inspired the Word and will reveal Himself in the Word. We must meditate on His Word. I recommend a careful reading of the 119th Psalm. Our difficulty and danger is that we put study ahead of meditation. Study is absolutely necessary, but meditation is also necessary. We must not only go to the Bible headfirst; we must also go to the Bible heart-first.

I got a letter today from Brazil from somebody I had never seen who commented about something I had written. "You put the emphasis on the Christian life as well as Christian truth. And the difficulty now, " said this person, "is that the emphasis falls on the Christian truth to the neglect of the Christian life."

If Christian truth does not produce Christian life, then there is something wrong with our finding that we call Christian truth. Christian truth must bring Christian life, and if we are going to have Christian life, we are going to have to nurture it with the dear old Book of God. I do not know how many times I have read it through, and I hardly ever try to really systematize. I have come heart- first and found in it all that my heart desires.

Lastly, cultivate the art of recognizing the presence of God everywhere. "Practice the presence," to use the phrase made famous by old Nicholas Herman.[4] Steal every moment you can to shoot a little prayer to God and remind Him that you love Him and you are His child. You are busy—awfully busy—but you are still His child.

Dr. A.B. Simpson gave us an illustration that I think is one of the finest in Christian literature. He said, "How can I pray without ceasing? It is obvious that I cannot kneel on my knees twenty-four hours a day for my lifetime. It is obvious that I cannot pray in the sense of addressing God formally all the time.

"But," he said, " 'Pray without ceasing' can be illustrated by the compass. The compass has a needle that has an affinity for the north magnetic pole, its home, and it wants to go that direction. It can be bumped, jostled, tossed and turned around artificially, but the main thing is, let it go and let it level off. It'll find its way pointing straight toward the north magnetic pole.

"So," he said, "in this life in which we live we will be busy doing this and that—the mother with her baby, the student with his book, the truck driver with his huge truck—we will have a thousand things to take our minds off God in the turbulence of life. The point is, just as soon as our mind is free, it flies back to its home again, back to God. If you think on God, that is praying without ceasing, keeping your heart free in God so that as soon as the pressure of daily living and studying and all the rest is off, the heart goes instantly to its home and to its God."

So, my friends, let us cultivate God; let us cultivate the Holy Spirit. Let us not be just two-thirds Trinitarians—let us be Trinitarians! Let us believe that God is. He subsists in three Persons, coexistent and co-eternal. The Father sent the Son to be incarnated and to die, and the Son and the Father sent the Holy Ghost to make the Father and the Son real.

We will never be alone, no matter where we are— never, never alone. The Christian will never be wholly lonely, for he has the presence of the Father and the Son within whispering distance of his heart all the time if he will agree to walk with God. To do so, he must agree to God's terms and follow at least this simple outline that I have given you tonight.

[Tozer delivered this sermon at Pierce Chapel, Wheaton College, on the night of October 3, 1952.]

The Danger of Being Almost Altogether

How good God has been to me to allow me to have such good friends. They say a friend is one who knows your faults and loves you anyway. When I comb over my memory and think of the good and great men that have adopted me, taken me to their hearts and allowed me to minister to their churches and schools, I simply do not know how I can thank God enough. It was most gracious for Dr. Edman to think of me here and have me here, along with Brother McAfee. I thank him for inviting me here. I have enjoyed myself and my preaching—I say that with no intention of being funny. I have preached about those things dear to my heart.

Tonight I want to talk about the danger of being "almost, but not altogether." Since the twenty-sixth chapter of Acts, in which this occurs, is thirty-two verses long and since I have a limited time, I shall not read the entire chapter. It is the story of Paul's defense before Agrippa. Let me break in at the twenty-second verse:

Having therefore obtained help of God, I continue unto this day, witnessing both to small and great, saying none other things than those which the prophets and Moses did say should come: That Christ should suffer, and that He should be the first that should rise from the dead, and should show light unto the people, and to the Gentiles. And as he thus spake for himself, Festus said with a loud voice, Paul, thou art beside thyself; much learning doth make thee mad. But he said, I am not mad, most noble Festus; but speak forth the words of truth and soberness. For the king knoweth of these things, before whom also I speak freely: for I am persuaded that none of these things are hidden from him; for this thing was not done in a corner. King Agrippa, believest thou the prophets? I know that thou believest. Then Agrippa said unto Paul, Almost thou persuadest me to be a Christian. And Paul said, I would to God, that not only thou, but also all that hear me this day, were both almost, and altogether such as I am, except these bonds. (26:22-29)

I would that you were not only almost, but altogether.

The living human scene here is one of almost ideal beauty and power. The witness of Paul before Agrippa is one of the noblest chapters in the entire Bible—and certainly in written literature.

Here is a man in chains, a victim of the spite and jealousies of Jews with connections. They had not the brass to charge him with a real crime. There were robbers there, but not a man rose to accuse Paul of robbery. There were murderers there, but no one charged this man with murder. There were traitors to their country, but no one dared say he was a traitor. There were arsonists there, but no one dared say, "This man burns down temples." Yet with one voice they cried against Paul. Here was a man of heaven among men of earth. With characteristic violence the men of earth reacted against the man of heaven.

As it is written in the Bible, the once-born man will persecute the twice-born man. Always it is Cain who will slay Abel. But here stands the man Paul to make his defense. I like to read this passage quietly and let it soak into my heart.

When Daniel Webster was holding audiences spellbound in this country with his amazing oratory, someone said, "I like to sit up close when Webster makes his speech. When I sit under that great brow and listen to the outpouring of his mighty eloquence I always go away feeling that I am a greater man than when I came in." And I like to read this passage sometimes just to see whether a bit of the wonder of it will not rub off on me— the superiority, the excellence of the man.

His whole bearing, his whole manner has no poor language but clean and right and good. It comes to us in this English that is beautiful and musical. His attitude, his diction—everything was sharp and clean and gracious. Here was a superior man. As he stands before the king to tell why he is there and defend himself, his argument is sound and learned and frank and direct. Nothing of the tricks of rhetoric that men employ—no appealing to the feeling of the man, but frankness and an honesty that goes straight through to the heart of the man, Agrippa. The substance of his testimony was such that it was, in itself, a tremendous argument for the message that he preached.

Notice he said that he had always been a strict religious Jew. He was no renegade, no man who had been careless about his relationship to God. He had been living in good conscience before God. Although, he admitted, blind on a point or two, he had always been a strict religious Jew, deeply schooled in the Old Testament itself and in the theology of the rabbis.

He then said that he had followed this Jewish religion that he had loved so much straight into the arms of Jesus. In embracing Jesus, he was not forsaking the religion of his fathers, but was helping to fulfill it. In coming to Jesus, he was coming to the One in whom all the prophets from the beginning of the world talked about.

Instead of apologizing for his conversion from Judaism to Christianity, he said, "I have never believed anything that is not believed by the fathers. I have never taught anything that is not written in the Scriptures of the very Jews who are opposing me and have me up here with chains on my wrists. The very religion my accusers hold and in whose name they have me here is the religion that I followed straight into the arms of Jesus Christ. So instead of apologizing for being a renegade Jew, I am a Jew who has found the Messiah, and the fulfillment of the prophesies of my fathers' Scriptures, which God has given through Moses and all the prophets."

He admitted frankly that at first, in his blindness, he had persecuted Christ. He had more knowledge than love or faith, so at first, he said, he had persecuted Christ. But he had met the Lord Jesus Christ on Damascus Road, and a flash of heavenly light had come to his soul—so blinding in its intensity he was sightless for three days.

"But now," he said, "I have a commission from God. Since that hour when I met God yonder on the road and stepped out from Judaism right straight on into Christianity and the arms of Christ, I have been preaching everywhere, witnessing only what the prophets have declared: that a Redeemer should suffer, die and rise again to be the light of the Gentiles and the Jews." Then dramatically he said, "It is for this reason that I have this chain on my wrist."

The man to whom he addressed these noble remarks was deeply moved. He had come from his busy life doing what kings are supposed to be doing, and now the sudden shock and wonder of it almost overcame him. For you see, Paul had indirectly set forth the powerful proof of the truth of Christianity, and he had also along with it indirectly set forth the reason why Agrippa should turn to Christ. The argument was, "If Jesus Christ is for me, He is also for you, O king. If I found Him by stepping over from Judaism into Christ, then that is an argument as old as Moses and older, so you ought also to be a Christian."

He did not say it quite like that, but the whole implication and inference is there. Agrippa was deeply moved by the preaching of the gospel, and he was not the only one. He said, "Almost thou persuadest me to be a Christian" (26:28). The different translations toss those words around, but they all add up to about the same thing. The man was profoundly touched, and he said, "I am near to believing what you have to say, Paul. Almost thou persuadest me."

Notice then that there was no quip in the mouth of Paul, and no flippant remark. He said, so nobly and so beautifully, "I wish before my God tonight, oh king, that you and all the others who are listening to me were not *almost* but *altogether* a Christian."

That is the reply of the man of God, and that is what I want to talk about—*I would that thou were not almost but altogether a true Christian*. There is a woe in the word "almost." When Agrippa used the word "almost," he did not know it at the time, but he had committed the greatest moral blunder of his life. History shows that the man's blunder was fatal.

Shipwrecks, earthquakes, tidal waves, epidemics and all the rest—nothing compares in sheer unrelieved tragedy with the soul that has seen the cross and turned away from it, that has heard the gospel and rejected it—maybe reluctantly and with many tears, maybe promising his own heart that he would not always reject it—but rejected it nevertheless. The moral tragedy of one who has finally decided that Jesus Christ is not for him—not all the great dramatists in the world, not Shakespeare nor Aeschylus nor any or all taken together could ever have packed into a drama all the stark terror and tragedy that is in the single word "almost" when it is not "altogether."

I think how this man had wiped out with this one word "almost." Kindly and friendly he was; I do not think there was even a sarcasm in his voice. He was deeply moved by the persuasion of the Word set before him. In refusing he wiped out forever all the dreams he ever had of a better world than this.

Regardless of our backgrounds I think there is hardly one who breathes with mortal breath that has not somewhere down the years said to himself, "This surely is not all there is to life. Surely these Christians and Jews and all the others who have dreamed about heaven—the American Indian with his 'happy hunting ground,' the Greek and his elysian fields— surely there must be something beyond all this. I cannot feed my soul on automobiles, television, bank accounts and good clothes and forget about it for another month, another year, another ten years."

Then in some moment of darkness or silence or at the graveside of a loved one, this feeling comes back again. "Oh," we say, "if there be a God, this

must not be it. There must be something real"—
and then to sell out that feeling! That is what
Agrippa did—he sold out.

Even that old king must have had his quiet moments there in the garden when he shooed away his
servants and sat in the silence, listening to the night
birds and dreaming of another world, of a hope beyond the grave. Perhaps he felt his pulse surging
within him and said, "It cannot always be, and when
it ends and there is no pulse, then where do I go?"

But he swept away all the hopes and the dreams
when he said "almost." All he had hoped for in the
future—the dreams and the longing for perma-
nence—all went out from under him and sus-
pended him in immensity without a foundation or
a place to rest or hide. Agrippa sold out before
God.

I think of others not so noble as Agrippa,
maybe simple people and plainer people like you
and me. I think of a man being tried for murder.
All the evidence is in and the jury retires as he
plays with his lead pencil and tries to keep up
his spirits by talking to his lawyer. He is waiting,
not knowing what to expect. Behind those
locked doors twelve men debate his future. You
seldom know what they say. Back there they toss
the evidence around, one man talking, then another. It looks as if the verdict is going to be "not
guilty." Then they decide, "Oh, it cannot be. The
evidence indicates guilt." Then, like a top that is
spinning and slowly running down, at last it all
goes one way and the vote is taken.

How near that man came to going out into the sunshine again, meeting his family again, sitting on his own lawn, reading the newspaper with his slippers on the floor! If he had only known, his heart would have stopped with the excitement of it. He was almost acquitted, but the vote was "guilty," and after months of waiting he pays the price. He walks into that room and sees the electric chair.

I once sat in that terrible chair. I walked up and allowed them to strap me in, and something of the horror of that moment came to my imagination. There he sits for one awful moment, and then it is over. He was *almost* a free citizen again.

I think of Judas Iscariot. I think that we overdo our description of Judas Iscariot. He was not a total devil. He was the son of perdition in the Hebrew sense, but it is an idiomatic expression, and it does not mean that he was a veritable devil. He had a heart too.

I do not believe in taking the heart out of people, not even the other political party nor the communists nor anybody. No matter how much the devil may get in and wreck and destroy and damn a man, he is still a human being. He may still love children, and he may still be friendly and have the dreams that Adam's sons have. Still he may love to hear the birds sing there on the bough and stroke the kitty as she goes by and call his dog and pat his head. He still may be a human being even though he is a Stalin or a Hitler.

I think Judas was a human being. We have made him a whipping boy and piled upon him all the evil that we can think about, and yet he was decent enough that nobody knew which one it was that betrayed Jesus with a kiss. If he had been such a devil they certainly would have said, "Oh, *Judas* did it," but nobody thought of Judas. Judas was secretly a bad man.

Certainly, no doubt, he had his good moments. We know this is so because after he betrayed Jesus with a kiss for thirty pieces of silver and found that Jesus had not escaped as he may have figured He would, but that his friend was actually going to die, he was overcome with remorse, not repentance. He rushed back and dramatically hurled down the $18 at the feet of the cynical priest and said, "I have betrayed innocent blood." And in a paroxysm of self-accusation he rushed out and hanged himself.

But he *almost* became St. Judas. He was *almost* a believer in Jesus, that is obvious. He loved that quiet, tender man who did and said such wonderfully strange and beautiful things, and though Judas did allow the devil to tempt him, that poor son of perdition did allow the perdition in his heart to damn him at last. He was not a damned man to start with, and he might have been St. Judas instead of Judas Iscariot.

The name whistles out of our mouths like the voice of a serpent. Nobody ever named his son Judas Iscariot Jones—nobody ever put that name upon an innocent brow of a baby, for he is Judas, the accursed, upon whom the ages have placed their stern disapproval. But it would have taken him only one minute to have become Judas the tender follower of Jesus, and maybe they would have put "Saint" before his name, but it was almost, not altogether. So he died with the curse on his head, so sorry for the way he had lived that he died of suicide.

I think of the life-term prisoners. For each one there must have been a time when he was almost all right. I believe in theological total depravity, that we are all bad, hopelessly bad, but I also believe that humanly there is a lot of good in folks. David said, "My goodness extendeth not to thee; but to the saints that are in the earth" (Psalm 16:2-3).

There are two directions of righteousness. Not everybody is a devil and has horns, though some evangelists try to make us think it so. But everybody is lost and has to be saved or they will be lost forever. There are lots of good, decent people that are not Christians, but that righteousness extends not to God, it extends out to people. It is a social righteousness, but that divine righteousness that makes us acceptable before the eyes of God must be given to us by the blood of the Lamb.

> When He shall come with trumpet sound,
> Oh may I then in Him be found;
> Dressed in His righteousness alone,
> Faultless to stand before the throne.[1]

That is the righteousness that admits me to the presence of God.

There is a righteousness that extends to my neighbor, a reputation I may get for being honest, decent, courteous, paying my debts, taking back the lawn mower and being a nice fellow among men. There is nothing wrong with that. There is a lot of modern preaching that sneers at righteousness and decency and good citizenship as though it were an affront to God to love your wife and pay your debts and bring your children up right. I think that is a tragic misunderstanding of this whole business to place a premium upon sin and penalize righteousness. No, the only problem is that this kind of righteousness is a social righteousness, and it goes out to men but not up to God.

There's many a life-term prisoner with the prison pallor upon his cheek who was once a decent fellow back home. I have never been committed to prisons but I have held meetings in prisons, and I have gone through and seen the men on death row waiting to die playing ball, trying to keep up their spirits a little. Those fellows were not all born bad. They were good, decent fellows around the house, no doubt like some of you, in fact all of us. We loved our mothers, teased our sisters and loved them to death though we would not let them know it.

Many of those boys who will die behind the dark prison walls at one time walked out of the house and down the street whistling. It was Sunday evening, and mother said, "Would you go to church with me tonight?"

"Oh, maybe, Mother; I will be back."

But he got out there, and a pal called him over with a whistle, and they went somewhere else. Nothing wrong with that. They missed church, but they went somewhere else. However, the next Sunday night they went still somewhere else, and it kept getting worse. Sin always gets worse by degrees. Not all sins are alike. Sin has intensity of guilt, pretty soon delinquency, then stolen cars and then murder. The life-term prisoner almost became a decent, respected citizen with a house on a lot, a car, family, lawn, a job, friends, vacations, fishing trips, ball games and fun. But tonight he is behind bars. It is not enough to be *almost* all right. "Oh," said the man of God, "I would that you might not only be almost but altogether."

I think of the living dead, the zombies and ghosts that walk. They may walk in expensive suits and drive luxury automobiles, but they are living dead men. Way back there yonder somewhere they had an opportunity. The gospel was preached, maybe by some simple man whose language was not too eloquent, but an honest man who loved his Savior and people. He heard it and walked away sober down the street, got in his car, and as he drove, he said to himself, "That man was right. I am a big fool to live the way I am living. He was right." He was almost, but not altogether. He said, "I will go back next Sunday night, that is what I will do," but next Sunday night his wife has a date for him someplace else and pretty soon he forgot his little vow. Now, older, he is a walking dead man. He is a disillusioned, embittered, defeated, lost man. Not a damned man yet, but a lost man. It is not enough to be almost.

I don't like to talk about hell. I said before that no man should preach about hell except with tears in his eyes. I trust there is tenderness at least in my heart, but I just want to mention in passing: I believe in hell.

I had a very dear friend when I was a lad. He taught me telegraphy, the old international Morse code, and this very dear friend and I went to a meeting together. He lied and said he was a Christian when a personal worker came and asked him if he was because he did not want them to bother him. Poor, miserable sinner that I was, at least I did not lie. I said, "No, I am not." Then they talked to me and pushed me around and massaged me and tried to get me to go, and I did not go, but at least I had not lied to the Holy Ghost.

Shortly after that my friend, still in his twenties, was sitting talking to his sister. He looked at his watch when the train whistled (he was a railroad man) and said, "Old Number Six is on time." Then he stopped talking and she wondered why, for he was a friendly, jovial fellow. She walked over, and he had died sitting there. He had evidently had some heart condition, and that was the last thing he ever said. Well, that struck me. You know how fellows in their teens get attached to some older man? Well, he was my hero. He was a railroad man, and I always loved the moan of the trains.

Trains and the sound of an old hound dog on the horizon are sweeter to me than symphony music. I would wake up in the night, and I knew the language of the whistle and knew what they were whistling about, and I knew my friend was gone forever. I knew where he had gone, and I myself was an unconverted sinner. I went to my room, got on my knees and prayed the most awful and futile prayer that I think has ever been prayed, to my knowledge. I prayed, "Oh God, please, if it is possible, get my friend Thurman out of hell." That is a terrible prayer. Of course God did not answer it. But Thurman was a nice fellow, a decent companion and a good man to be around, and he was *almost* saved.

Thurman is not here anymore. God is going to do something to take the sadness and sting out of those friends and family members that you wept over who died without Christ. In that great day when God wipes tears away, He will wipe those tears away too (Revelation 21:4). I am sure of that.

Yet down on the human level, you still grieve for that nice brother whom you loved, who used to baby-sit you before the term "baby-sitting" was heard of, who gave you his clothes when he outgrew them, who let you ride his bicycle—and who died suddenly, and died without Christ. You have grieved ever since. He was a decent fellow and your loved brother, but he is gone; you know where he has gone and not all the kindness of the preacher can ever get him out of there. God handles men when they die.

He was a good fellow, and there is many a man like that down there. If we were to go to that terrible place (and I am as near to it as I ever want to get), we would find lots of people who can quote Scripture. We would find people who would astonish us preachers with the number of verses and texts they could quote. If there would be such a thing as singing, though there could not be, I am sure that there are tens of thousands there that could join us in singing "Amazing grace, how sweet the sound," though it would not apply to them.

The people who are there are not all pagans, Nazis and communists. People that are there, many of them, are people that *almost* did not go there. *Almost* they escaped it. *Almost* they sought God. They planned, maybe, and promised. They walked around a church two or three times and started in, and then backed off and did not go in. Maybe they sat through many a revival meeting and promised themselves, but they did not do anything about it. Almost is not enough.

Are you a true Christian? Please do not take me wrongly and be hurt by this. I must discharge my soul before God. Are you a true Christian?

Some of us, particularly young people, are being badly betrayed these days by our teachers, church people and folks who preach and teach like myself. We do not mean to do it, but we are so eager to make a convert that we sometimes rush people prematurely into a decision which never goes deep enough. We get them to sign a tract or sign a New

Testament. I do not mean that is not a good thing to do, but many times it misfires and does not get the sinner in at all. Sometimes they stand and say, "Yes, I take Him," but they do not know what they have stood for. They go out unchanged and do not know quite why.

My listening friends, if this is the last time you ever hear my voice, hear me say this to you, that unless you have been changed by an inner working of God in your heart, in what we call regeneration, you are still in your sins. No amount of baptizing or going to church or joining religious groups or reading New Testaments—no amount of religious effort can save your soul. "Except a man be born again, he cannot see the kingdom of God" (John 3:3).

Being born again does not mean signing your name on a card, though if you are born again you can sign your name on a card, thank God. Mail it in and say, "I am born again." I do not mean to speak against that, I only say that many times that does not go far enough. In our eagerness to count noses and say we had forty conversions yesterday, we let people through when in honesty to their soul we never should have done it.

Come on, you young people, all of you. God bless you! I have watched your faces, you have nodded and said "Hi" to me as I walked around the campus, and I suppose you thought, "What an old fellow that is." Maybe you did not admire me, but oh, how I have admired you! A lot of you remind me of my kids, my little girl and what she will be four or five years from now when she comes to Wheaton. And I have loved you.

Though our campaign has been more of a deeper- life conference than an evangelistic campaign, I cannot close without saying to you, please do not ever let the devil fool you. Do not rest with "almost." Make it "altogether." Be sure that you are all the way in—that Jesus Christ is yours and you are His.

You say, "How can you know, Mr. Tozer?" Well, you meet all the biblical conditions there are and trust Him, and your trust will be its own reward. His work within you will be self-validating and self-witnessing, and you will know you have passed from death unto life. And do not forget, you *can* know it! Do not let yourself be cheated, please, because the man of God said, "It is not enough to be almost, but you must be altogether."

I thank God my conversion was a real, transforming, amazing conversion that turned me from being a careless sinner to being a Christian and I knew that I was born again. I did not have to be told it—I knew. It was not a conclusion I had drawn from a set of texts. It was partly that, certainly, for faith cometh by hearing the Word of God (Romans 10:17), but it became to me more than that. It became for me an inner witness—I am His and He is mine. "Amazing love, how can it be?"

You can know tonight. Think for a moment about your own heart. Are you a true Christian— an "altogether" Christian? Or are you *almost* converted? Will you not make this the time when you say, "I do not care what anybody says: I am going to push my way through past all my fears and doubts to Jesus Christ, and I am going to throw myself out on Him like I would throw myself off a diving board into a swimming pool. I will trust Him tonight to save me through and through. May it not be said of me in that terrible day, 'You were almost in, but not altogether.' " No greater tragedy could visit you—polio, the loss of arms or legs, blindness—nothing could be so starkly frightful as your having been almost but never really born again by faith in Jesus Christ.

[This sermon was delivered at Wheaton College's Pierce Chapel on the evening of October 5, 1952.]

CHAPTER

11

Is God Enough?

Here is an idea advanced by an old man of
God 2,500 years ago, as recorded in Jeremiah
6:16. "Thus saith the LORD, Stand ye in the ways,
and see, and ask for the old paths, where is the
good way, and walk therein, and ye shall find rest
for your souls." That is all but one line of the six-
teenth verse. The other line I wish were not there,
but it is: "But they said, We will not walk therein."

This text must be seen in its historic context. Israel was in grave physical danger for moral reasons. They had left the old paths and the old ways
and had blasted out a shortcut for themselves that
was rapidly taking them into quicksand and death,
and Jeremiah offered to come to their rescue. He
said, "If you want to escape what is ahead for you,
ask for the old paths and turn onto the old paved
highway that God has made for you, and you will
come out all right." But Israel did not listen.

The reason Israel was in trouble was that she
had gotten tired of God. This had not been the first
time. Once, on the mount, Moses, their leader—
whom they rallied to because he was trustworthy,
visible and exercised leadership—went out of their

159

sight for a while. Because they could not get their
eyes on anything and could not touch anything,
they had not the inward stability and stamina
enough to wait for God's time. God was not
enough for them, so they made themselves a gold-
en calf.

It happened again in the wilderness later, after
they had eaten manna from heaven ("angels' food"
it says in Psalm 78:25) and got tired of that diet.
Although manna had everything they needed, they
demanded to have something a bit more spicy.
Consequently, God sent them flesh, but He sent a
blight along with it.

This was the outcropping of a natural, though
sinful, tendency in humanity. It is a bad streak in
human nature which finds goodness boring. We
get tired of it after a while, and the only way we
can endure it is to mix it with something highly
spiced.

I think I have gotten to the bottom of the trouble
today in modern conservative Christian circles of
which you and I, of course, are a part and would
not be anything else. But there are serious difficul-
ties that some of us are seeing, and I believe the
root and bottom of it all is that many of us have
become bored with God.

We have not the courage of the atheist who
bares his breast to the high heavens and demands
that if there be a God, He strike him dead. We
want the safety of the cross, and yet we are not satisfied with the cross. We want the protecting wing
of God, provided God will allow us a certain num-

ber of childish toys that we may be able to play with to keep our juvenile minds occupied while we go our way. We invent to ourselves instruments of music like David (figuratively speaking). We have a multitude of trifles to make up for the fact that God is not enough for us.

For many Christians it is a fact that God is not enough. Indeed, there is nobody quite so eloquent as one who is busy arguing in favor of extras and additions that have no place either in the Old or New Testaments or in the traditional Church of Christ. Nobody can get quite so eloquent as the man who has found that God is not enough and who has to have something to add to God to satisfy his poor heart.

Those who gaze homesick toward the mount and desire a view of God in the fire, who wish to push into the Presence of the Holy God and stand in awful silence there—satisfied as the angels in heaven, as the cherubim before the throne and as the saints of the ages, satisfied with what God is— are considered to be radicals, extremists, fanatics, killjoys and a good many other names not quite so complimentary. Nevertheless, I joyfully put myself over on their side and say that I believe that we will not be where we ought to be until we get to a place where God is enough for us.

We all have to live in the world. We even have to live in the twentieth century, believe it or not. There is no avenue of escape just yet. But it is one thing to accept the twentieth century with its multitude of gadgets, sanctifying and making them necessary for our spiritual happiness; it is quite another to live as though we were not in the world at all. From this latter perspective people live where thoughts of God are enough to nourish their minds for days on end. A minute of experience with the Presence of God brings more delight to them than all the invented gadgets in the world! Between those two views there is a great gulf fixed, but a bored and blasé generation does not want to hear anything about the old paths. Scripture says, "Seek the old paths" (see Jeremiah 6:16).

There are two errors that are pretty current with regard to old things. The first is that everything old is good, and everything new is bad. That idea, of course, is held by some people, and it harms progress and discourages all thought. It also petrifies the imagination and digs a grave for all expectation. I am afraid that in our evangelical circles, when it comes to theology and spiritual thought, we have adopted the notion that the old is good and that everything new is bad in the realm of theology and spiritual ideas. We have to go back to John Bunyan or somewhere way back yonder to discover a man who has spiritual imagination enough even to state things differently from that which is current in his time.

I will tell you what I would like to see for this critical age. I would like to see come out of this student body (and others like it all over the world) a number of persons committed to the everlastingness of the truth as it is given from heaven, manifested in the inspiration of Scripture and the

faith of our fathers. I would like to see you committed to this truth, world without end, with your
bridges burnt behind you so that it is impossible to
go back theologically from this evangelical position. Then, before God Almighty, I would hope to
see you full of the Spirit, with a Spirit-filled intellect immersed in the truth.

The result would be the truth related in an
imaginative way for our time. Truth would have
that purpose and imaginative power that would
enable us to show surprise and wonder when we
talk about the things of God. We have lost that in
religious ideas. Consequently, we have had to
make up for our lack of wonder, surprise and
"zing" by dragging in 10,000 things that God never
intended should be dragged in at all. Therefore, it
is often very difficult to tell whether we are in the
Church of God or at some amusement park.

The second error, which we also strangely enough
embrace, is that everything new is good and everything old is bad. That view has to do with our *practice* of religion. When it comes to our *beliefs*, we
accept the doctrine that what our bearded fathers believed about a text is all there is to it, and that there is
not anything else that can be said on the subject. All
we have to do is have a good memory, remembering
what Dr. So-and-so said about it, because memory is
the only faculty of the religious mentality that is
working much now. We try to remember what the fathers said about a text, but we bring no imagination,
no fresh life, no fresh touch to the development of it
ourselves.

The error that everything new is good and everything old is bad takes place in the realm of practice and worship and religious activity generally. This is a view—if I can sanctify or dignify it with the word *view*—of the partly educated or the badly educated (I do not know which would be worse), of the intellectually vain and the worldly, of the carnal man who has not the Spirit. Such are the unstable and the impatient, the bored and the contemptuous. It can lead, of course, to great rebellion against the truth. If the idea that everything new is good and everything old is bad gets into theology, it makes modernists out of us. If this notion gets into fundamental circles, it makes fools out of us, and there is a great deal of it throughout the country.

What is the way? The way is given to us here by the Holy Ghost: "Stand in the way, and see for yourselves, and ask for the old paths, the good way, and you shall find rest to your souls" (see Jeremiah 6:16). What shall we find in these good old paths? We will find everlasting truths. We will find what may be called the primary grounds, the irreducible elements, those things that are neither new nor old; they are ancient and eternal and have no time quality attached to them at all.

The great doctrines of the Bible are not timely. When a man comes up to me and says, "Mr. Tozer, that was a timely sermon," I take it as a doubtful compliment, for the truths of God are not timely (that is, geared into time). The truths of God are eternal. They rise above time, and they were as true when Adam was in the garden as they will be true in the millennium or in the ages that follow.

There are certain great truths: God, God's creating us, our response and relation to God, human sin, human redemption, the incarnation, the indwelling Christ, the union of the soul with the Triune God. All these are great eternal truths, true under all kinds of conditions, among all people everywhere and in every age in the world, no less true and no more true because they are absolutely true. Indeed, we will never be where we should be until these become to us the source of thrill. The entertainment of great spiritual concepts will lift us like a song until, brooding upon the great ideas of the Triune God and all He means to us, will thrill us like a stimulant from within.

We will never be where we ought to be until we go back to those old paths and learn to find God. We will cease to be bored with God. We will cease to make His redemptive plan merely an escape from hell and put the thought of hell and all that way behind us in the dim, disappearing past. Instead, we will center our affections upon God and Christ, where Christ sits at the right hand of God, and become specialists and experts in the realm of the spiritual life.

It is amazing how little outside stimulus we need if we have that inward stimulus. It is amazing how much God will meet our needs. It will not be God *and* something else. It will be God *every-*

thing. And then, wisely, we will gear into our times, and we will gear into the gadgets around us, and we will gear into the needs of others, and in a moment we will become as practical as overshoes and as alert to the needs of the world around us as the most keen sociologist. Nevertheless, at the same time our great anchor will be God above. And if at any moment we should be cut off from our environment so that we did not have the stimulation and comfort of what the world provides, we would still be perfectly restful, for God would be enough.

This is where we should seek to be, and I do not think this is too heavy a burden for you young people. I think youth will respond to the right leadership if it is given them, so I deliberately turn your minds to the old paths—not the old beards and the old clothes nor the old ideas, but to the ancient and eternal truths which our fathers have given and which the Scriptures contain. Then from there on we will know God and Christ in increasing intimacy as the years go by, and we will find heaven drawn near and earth receding as we get older. May God give us the courage to be obedient to His truths in this tragic, critical and dangerous hour in which we live.

[Tozer preached this sermon in Wheaton College, Pierce Chapel, on the morning of March 4, 1954.]

ENDNOTES

Chapter 1 - Spiritual Power

[1] William Jennings Bryan (1860-1925). A career politician and leading Christian layman.

Chapter 2 - Preparing the Way for the Lord

[1] A.B. Simpson (1843-1919). The celebrated writer and founder of The Christian and Missionary Alliance.
[2] Charles Wesley (1707-1788). One of the greatest hymn writers of all time.
[3] Hymn by Charles Wesley, "Arise, My Soul, Arise! ", 1742.
[4] Raymond McAfee, Tozer's associate pastor, music director, and long-time friend.

Chapter 3 - Grieve Not the Holy Spirit

[1] Blasphemy against the Holy Spirit is also found in Luke 12:10.
[2] Hymn by Mrs. A.A. Whiddington, "Not I, But Christ," refrain.
[3] Hymn by George Matheson, "O Love That Wilt Not Let Me Go," stanza 4.

Chapter 4 - The Enemy Within

[1] Frederick William Faber (1814-1863).

Chapter 5 - Wounds from God

[1] Soren Kierkegaard (1813-1855).
[2] The Korean War (1950-1952) was still raging on.
[3] Dwight L. Moody (1837-1899). The American evangelist did say this.
[4] George Mueller (1805-1898). A Christian leader who was best known for founding orphanages and schools in England. His autobiography, *A Life of Trust*, was a Christian best- seller.

Chapter 6 - Five Keys to the Faithful Christian Life

[1] Most likely referring to Winona Lake Bible Conference, winona Lake, Indiana.
[2] The radio station of Moody Bible Institute, Chicago, Illinois.
[3] This is a reference to a speech delivered by Vice Presidential candidate Richard M. Nixon during the 1952 Presidential campaign. Nixon was charged with using campaign funds for personal use. In his famous "Checkers Speech," he told the public he was going to set aside pretense and politics and simply pour out the truth from his heart.
[4] *Wingspread (Camp Hill, PA: Christian Publications, 1943), is a biography of A.B. Simpson written by Tozer. It is still in print.*

Chapter 7 - How to Be Filled with the Holy Spirit

[1] Hymn by Frederick W. Faber, "O Jesus, Jesus."

Chapter 8 - Be Filled with the Spirit

[1] Dr. V. Raymond Edman (1900-1967) was president of Wheaton College from 1941 to 1964. He was on the platform with Tozer when this message was delivered.

Chapter 9 - How to Cultivate the Spirit's Companionship

[1] Samuel Pepys (1633-1703), whose diary is a window on the last part of the seventeenth-century in England.
[2] John Steinbeck (1902-1968), winner of the 1962 Nobel prize for literature. He is best known for his novel *The Grapes of Wrath.*
[3] Paul Rader (1879-1938), pastor of Chicago's Moody Church and a well-known radio evangelist.
[4] Nicholas Herman (c. 1605-1691), better known as Brother Lawrence, author of *The Practice of the Presence of God.*

Chapter 10 - The Danger of Being Almost Altogether

[1] Hymn, "My Hope Is Built on Nothing Less," verse 4; text by Edward Mote, 1797-1874.

Other titles by A.W. Tozer
published by Christian Publications:

Order Tozer books from
Christian Publications' web page at
www.cpi-horizon.com